ALL MY BAD HABITS
poetry

(✱) **green**hill

https://greenhillpublishing.com.au/

William, Curtis (author)
All My Bad Habits
ISBN 978-1-923265-42-4 (paperback)
POETRY

Typeset Calluna Regular 10/14pt
Cover and book design by Green Hill
Photography by Joshua Turner from JT Photographic Studios

ALL MY BAD HABITS

poetry

curtis william

To the people with shattered edges, the hopeless romantics and those who battle their bad habits. This is for you. May this poetic journey take you through the waves and motions of this crazy world we live in. Come alone and witness the thrill of growing up. I hope somewhere you find peace on the road less travelled by.

Thank you,

To my dear friends Alex, Josh, Jai, Laura, Rhiannon, Jess, Jayme, Gabbi, Craig, Jade, Elise and all the rest I say thank you for putting up with me while I put this together with a broken heart. Never once did you judge me, you just let me create. What a beautiful gift your friendship is. Mum and Dad, thank you for making me the man I am who wears his heart on his sleeve and knows his power. Of course, Erin, Chris, and Lyn, I must thank you for exposing me to the world of writing and showing me how to craft in a way that harnesses my voice. English teachers are truly the gift that keeps on giving, thank you. To everyone who said kind words amidst my pain, smiles, and moments of self-loathing, thank you for showing me the world is even bigger than I realised.

Finally, to the boy who broke the poet's heart, thank you too. There has and always will be love there for you too.

All my love, and all my bad habits

"Here's to my love. O true apothecary,
Thy drugs are quick. Thus with a kiss I die"
ROMEO AND JULIET, ACT V, SCENE III

WHEN I STARTED WRITING

From the start of *All My Bad Habits* I was unsure of the direction it would take and what it would become. The journey started days before a trip to the United States with my friend Jessica, when the idea of travel became a nostalgia inducing flood of memories. Upon witnessing a New York City Christmas, I fell in love with the idea of love again. I remember making a wish in Times Square on a piece of paper that would be dropped in the streets on New Year's Eve. As sad as it sounds, I wished for something that I thought would complete me as a person. I wished for *someone to love me*. Little did I know that sometimes wishes come true, at a price. I met people who sent sparks into my heart. I began to work on my mind and body to restore a sense of pride and confidence in myself. I had never been better; I grew a better relationship with myself and started healing old wounds, forming good habits, and falling in love with life again. Then one night, we passed in the hallway light.

And everything would change.

Part One

OLD HABITS

Sunday

Your lips, I bet, taste like fresh orange juice;
Bitter.
Where the glass meets my lips,
I yawn and pat my pretty face,
But the rim is still tainted.

In Passing

I can't tell the difference between chance and fate;
Both happen before I can even blink.

It's all the same to me,
Like the dreams I have about you in the middle of the night;
They bring me closer to you.

Missed Moment

Just
One
      Missed
            Moment

And you wouldn't be mine.

Closer

Your head buried in the pillow,
Was edging closer to my side of the bed.

Both times we've met, my shoulder hurt,
Twisted and turned,
Pressure points picked me out,
And my body ached
From keeping it upright in the middle of the night.
It's a balancing act.

Your soft breath against my skin,
Could colour my world,
In shades I cannot see with anyone.
One huff of sleepy slumber sends my skin into goosebumps,
A blow that boulders down feather towers.

But while I let you rest,
I will remain upright for both of us.

Cramped

Single beds,
　　　Soft breaths,
　　　　　Kind words,
　　　　　　　Pressed together.
　　　　　　　Cramped.
Our little love language.

The Trials

I stand before my sin and take an oath for truth.
I drank my cologne-scented poison despite my own head.
The judge whispers,
But I plead innocent to the case of Head vs Heart;
Not in my favour.
My evidence of good intentions and promises of talk therapy
    fall short.
The jury of forgotten oaths stand before me,
The barrister bows his head,
Sentenced to walk the road most travelled by.

Thanks

I can pluck emotions like goose feathers,
Read, rip, and respond,
Like knives and letters.
Oh, how easily they spill their contents.

Dolly-Do

He was my partner in crime,
We were a duo like no other,
Could have been best friends till time ends,
But good things rarely last forever.

He sat on a couch in my old apartment,
Sobbing in self-loathing and boy, could I understand his
	heartache,
We shared beds as kids,
Houses as adults,
Memories in the car,
Drinks in foreign bars,

Now we hardly speak, it's okay, really,
Because he's getting married
Living the life he's always wanted,
I'm so happy he found peace.

Each to their Own

You're the slow speakeasy's last call for drinks,
                 I'm the midday festival with vibrations
                 you can feel in your chest
Like sour soju
                 Or smooth whiskey,

    Each has a place in this world, and each is for us.

Bro

Call me

        Bro

           The same way I'd call you

                    Mine.

Sunday (again)

I want sleepy Sundays. The ones where your head digs into
   my shoulders.

                                              I can't sleep.
So I wake up and make us breakfast. Rest your head,
I'll take it from here.

Golden Boy

He's the kind of purity that makes this world a wonderful
    place to exist in,
The purity that helps an old and grey lady in the garden,
The purity that stops to chat to everyone he knows,
Selflessness is in his nature,
Helpfulness is his way of nurture,
The purity that couldn't hurt a soul even if he wanted to,
The purity that is a blessing we never give thanks for.

Way Back When

I watch my life backwards,
                    Fast forward,
And the video gets jammed like a 90's VHS.
                                Flicker
                                        Flicker
                                                Flicker
                                                        On the same
                                                            Frame.
The scene whereby chance we first met, passing through a
    hotel hallway
City lights, camera, action,
                        The Start of Act III

Mean It

I want you genuinely.
Not the half-hearted kiss from a relative,
Nor the warm beer at lockout,
Nor the last stop before the freeway.

I want you like we want
      Summer,
      Cold beers,
      Adventure,
         Or simply no place to be.
I want simple and effortless beauty.

Skin Mark

You leave a mark on me
Like an ink stain,
A deep, saturated mark.
It's not a wound leaving scars,
                              But rather, pretty pictures.
The raised lines map our way.
Because ink stains are pretty,
When you're the artist all over me.

Bold

It's my turn,
> To make you,
>> Feel something.

Tortured Poet

Like a tortured poet,
I spill my guts. An inkwell of
                    Thoughts
                      And
                        Truths.

Stay

When raindrops are cold and you're shivering,
I'll pop open an umbrella.
    You
Can stand next to me,
Until the clouds go away.
     Or stay
       Even after the rain.

Sorry I'm Anxious

Anxious stress, I could write a book about all this mess.
I'd give you my warmth, give you my best,
But after years of mapped treasures,
What I realised was utopia.
Sailing the seas just isn't for me.

Morning

Moan me my good mornings under the grumble of tired
   breaths.
When clouds are stark and grey,
I'll make you a cup of coffee.
You
    Toss
        And
            Turn.
                Wait
And ask me to stay.

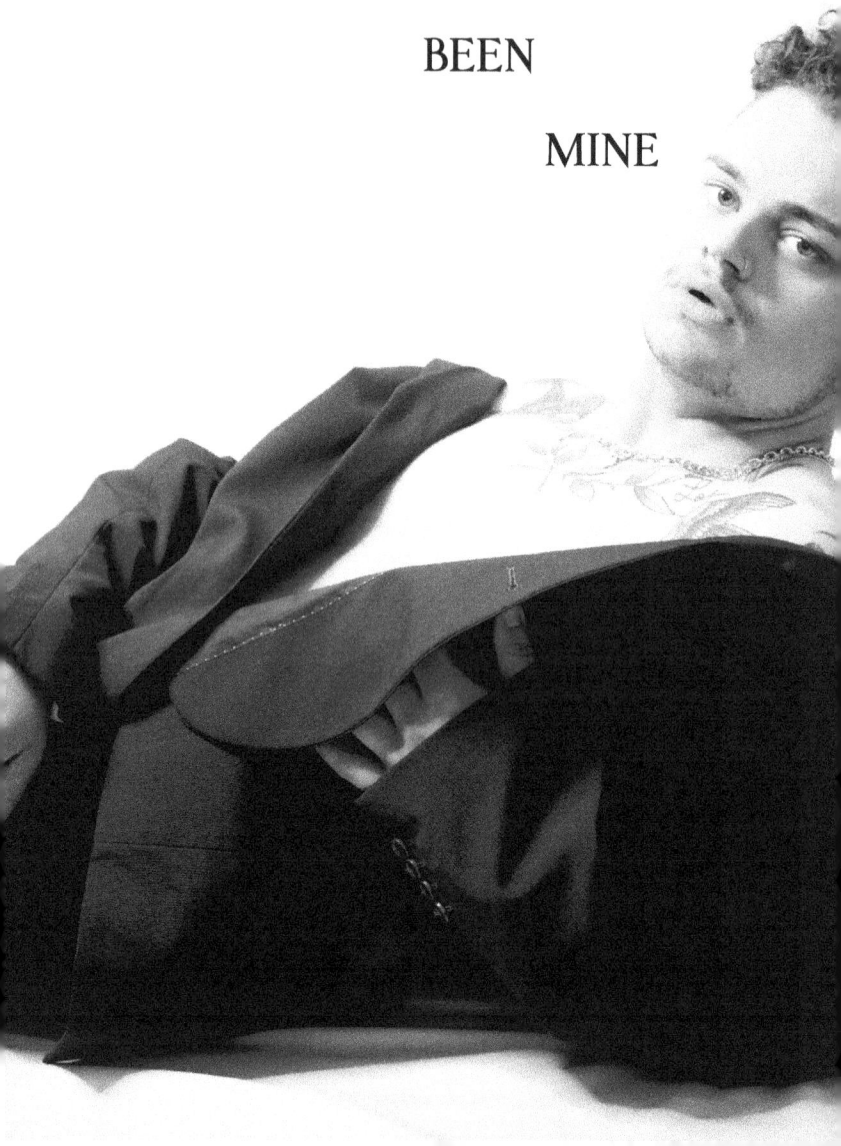

ONE

MISSED

MOMENT

AND YOU WOULD'VE NEVER

BEEN

MINE

It's Cold in London

What once was fate, a warm hand,
Which was feeding me your invisible string,
Is now the double-edged fork,
Stuck in the road.

I am doomed if I do,
            I am doomed if I go,
So long London,
            My colours have been shown.

For You

Loving you ruined everything,
                    In the best way possible.

Long Live London

So long London,
                    Maybe one day,
Soon,
I'll call your cobblestones "home".

Falling

Falling in love is like a whirlwind at the beginning
   of our first flight.
The clouds and cities underneath paint pretty pictures of
The lives we make, the hearts we break,
The risks worthy of taking,
And the life we've dreamt of making.

Life With You

I want your late nights at the bar,
I want your sleepy Sunday mornings
Where there's nothing much we need to do.
I want those fights that would end others
    but make us stronger.
I want those flirtations, not knowing if they'll end here
    or in my bedroom,
I want moments with you eating shitty catered food in a
    crowded room,
I want us to be proud of each other,
I want to be a team.

Private Matters

The secret they didn't see light up my phone,
The fingers pressed on my collarbone,
The lips of a boy I barely know,
Why with him, does it feel so real?

What's Next?

It's a thrill that keeps you alive,
Not knowing what's next.
It's in those moments you remember that this world offers us
Chances, people, and moments,
All at our doorstep,
Reminding us that anything is possible.

Dear Little Me

Sometimes,
When I am eating dinner,
Or making my bed,
Showering,
And cursing my own name,
I remember wishing I was nicer to him.

He was hurt enough.

Pod Guy

New Year, new fear,
I didn't know where I'd be,
But that all changed one night
Come February.

Your hands, your lips
Are all over me.
I drew stars, leaked scars,
When come March
It was all about you and me.

Who knew, it'd be true
The boy of my dreams,
Was waiting for me in Sydney?

Being Here

I'm glad you're here,
So you can feel that special kind of something,
The warmth you get when
You just fucking know.

I'm glad you're here, of all the places you could have been.

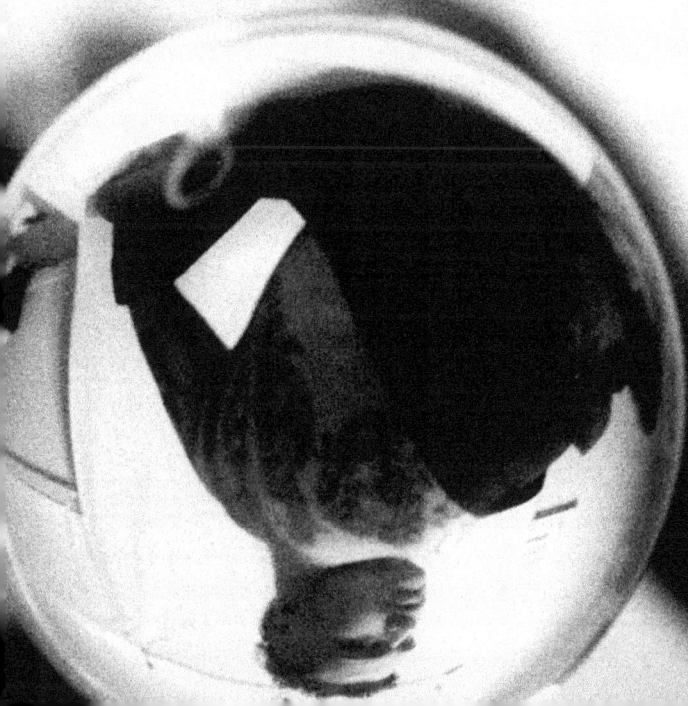

MEETING YOU

TURNED

MY

WHOLE

WORLD

Snooze

Your back curves like coastal sand dunes,
I'm sailing your smooth edges across unlikely grains,
Carefully, I move past the creeps and critters,
The rock in my waters wave goodbye,
But like the tide, I cannot resist you till noon.

WYKYK

Sometimes you just know.
Eyes meet and it's like taking flight,
By surprise.
C'mon, let's give them a show!
Dance with me!
When
      You
Know
      You
Know.

Just a Sydney Haiku

City nights run cool,
Looking over dreamscape scenes,
And you were with me.

Lucky

You are like a lottery ticket fluttering between commuters.
Everybody wants you.
If I got you, they would still go to great lengths to have you
Fuelled by all those who wield bad intentions.
Not commonly encountered, but now and again someone
   has to get lucky.
And today, that is me.

Question

I didn't know if you knew,
With you I'd start something new,
Did I come on strong too soon?
Or did I do what I always do?

The Morning After the Parade

The morning came and
I sat on a train,
In last night's outfit
Thinking
I just met the love of my life.

That Feeling

Being out hits differently as a pair.
I'm not walking alone.

We're a team
                Between clinked drinks,
With chosen family;
                You and me.

Good Enough Alone

Wouldn't it be nice to love unconditionally,
    Without the *chokehold* of anxious thoughts
Or hyper fixations?
             Just
                Let
                  It
                    Be.

Another Love Haiku

Go and make your mark
But use your finest colours.
Maybe then I'll know.

In My Pocket

You make me want you in ways where
Getting nothing back is still somehow a win.
Place the hotel key in my pocket,
My expired coupon,
Crumped
In my pocket,
Forgotten.

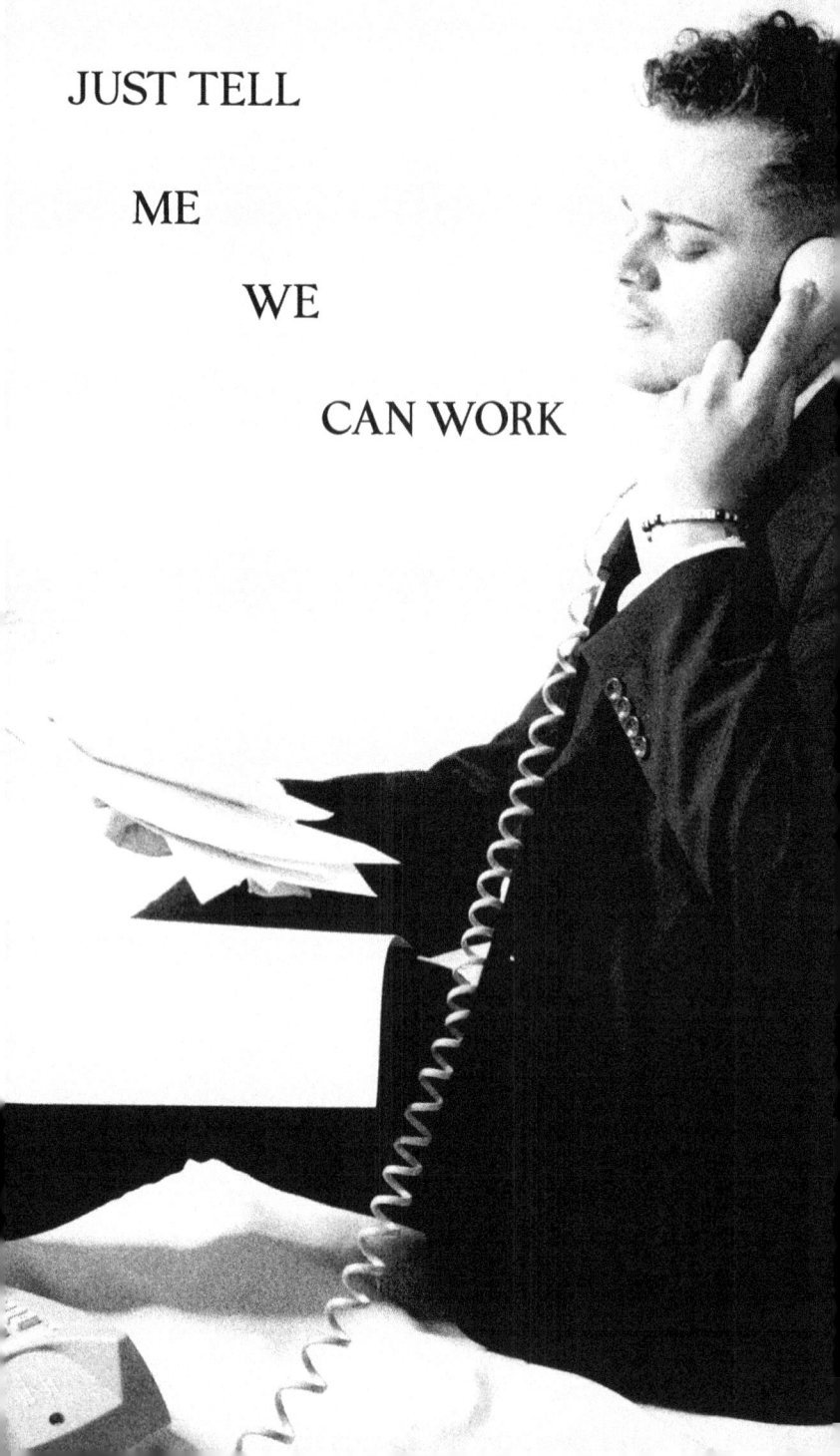

Pod Guy (Part 2)

Meeting you caught me off guard, like when someone buys
    your drink without you asking.
As you sat beside me, your hands were fumbling for a missed
    door key,
Your green eyes were locked in with a country smile.
As you sat beside me, your head was turning.
"You wanna come drink with us?" you asked.
"Yes," I replied, the easiest I've ever nodded in my life.

We gazed over the rooftop and sank soju,
Your head turned in a moment alone.
"I think you're cute," left your lips.
You made a move, as quickly as I could.
I knew it'd be you.
A proposition?
That green hat, I brushed back from your head so I could kiss
    you.
Now that's making a move.

When the morning came, we were drenched in the sunlit
    haze,
Of smiles and hands in our hair.
Never leave this bed.
In fact, never leave again.

Please Be Patient

I know I'm overdramatic,
I get it from my mother.
It's the one switch I can't flick off.
I'll defend myself like a knight in a kingdom battle.
I don't think I ever learned how to not spit acid words,
Surviving from the skin of my teeth
Damage on the enamel.

Am I 'that' Kid?

Life feels safe with you, as I sip coffee by the window.
I wonder,
Is this the normal I never felt?
Like when you go to friends' houses and their parents are
    sober and calm,
Or when you go to a birthday party and the kids are walked
    inside,
How about after-school jitters?
Do you not get anxious at 4pm?

You bring safety to a world I didn't know existed above the
    bridge,
People who talk things over, with no walkouts or
    breakdowns,
Trust me when I say that with you in my life, I have brighter
    days.

What must it have been like to grow up in a world that's
    beautiful?

Dear Best Friend

After the big parties,
The night ends,
And we walk home
With life and friends.

On warm days,
In sunshine,
Messy nights,
Cab rides,

Rosé is flowing,
Games night,
I saved you a seat,
Because it's our life.

You're my whole world.
It's how our story ends,
It's you and me.
You're my best friend.

The Complex

Imagine having a good thing happen to you,
And not a single part of you thinks you deserve it.

Imagine all those muddled nights of drunken slurred words,
The sickening sweet scent of anger,
Bitter betrayal and words with meanings unforgiven.

Neither of them will remember in the morning,
The pain they carry in packed luggage on the living room
    floor.
One nasty comment made,
Can cast stones in my bag,
And now I will carry it on my back.

Anxiety (Again)

I'm fucking anxious all the damn time.
One thoughtless sentence leads me down the rabbit hole of
    distrust,
That even the most noble of claws cannot dig out of.
I know it's my problem to work through.
Boy, I am tired,
But I smile, sip my caffeine, and get to work.
Giving up on him is giving up on you,
And giving up on you is giving up on me.
All of these treasures are worth the extra mile on the tricky
    road to travel.

Healing Me

Hurt people, hurt people.
There's no excuse for that
But when I think I have reason to attack,
A small, firm hand pulls me back.
The hurt boy takes the wheel and spits insults like a snake.
Disappointment and denial become flames of fire.

I stand now fully grown, and aware of his presence.
He is tired, he needs to rest.
I am grown up now, and I can look after both of us.
I grasp my shoulder, hoping he feels it.
Sit back, you're alright.
I've got us for the rest of our time.

Taken

"I will be telling people I'm taken," are words that left your
    lips.
You said I had to trust more openly,
But the spies who come in from the cold of my heart
Are spread with scepticism.
Will you really tell people that?
And if you do, are you taken by me?

Worst of You

Go ahead,
                    And give me
     Nothing.
I'll say something back.

Between Worlds

Every now and again, I picture my other choices,
My boots against the cobblestone.
They don't shine quite the same in gloomy clouds
And don't make that clicking sound I love in the pattern
    of rain.

The western ground kicks against my feet,
I'm walking myself home to you,
That choice made all the difference.

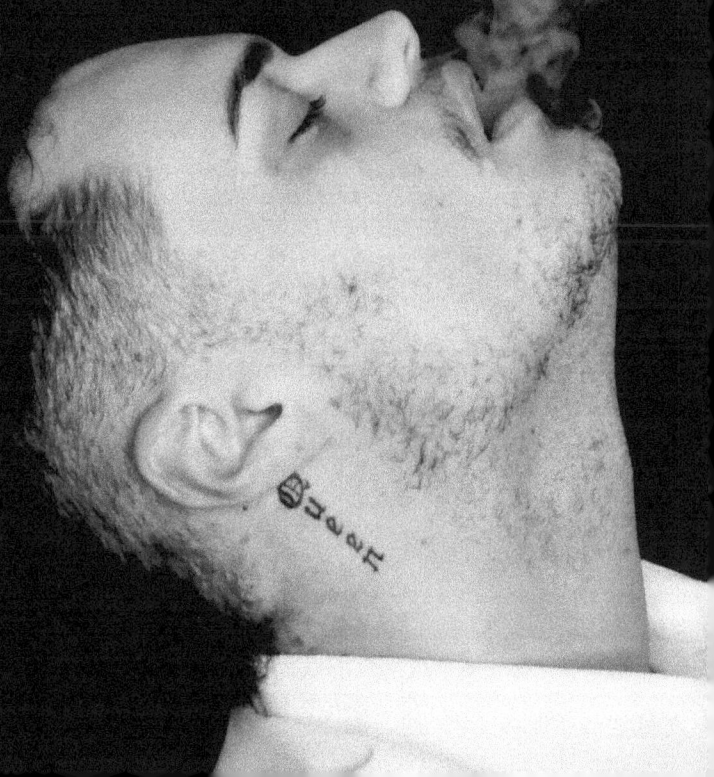

LET ME BREATHE YOU IN LIKE NICOTINE GIVE ME THAT HEADSPINE

Trespassing Thoughts

Now that I know your lips,
And your body,
The idea of someone else trespassing on your skin
Makes my spine chill.

What a deceitful dance with the devil temptation must be.
Hell freezes over the day I give in to not loving you,
I'd double-cross my own heart,
Duplicitously impersonate my own state of mind
Just to keep you away from enemy lines,
But if everyone else wants you,
Falling feels like jumping.

Change is a Thing

The sinking feeling of everything coming down around me,
Makes my head spin,
And the world would.
There's a negative charge that runs between the beats of my
    heart.
But nothing is the same, and nothing ever will be
And it never was.

Road trip

Let's go.
Nowhere in particular,
Just two found souls behind the wheel looking for
   somewhere
And each other all at the same time.
The service station snacks, your music choices.
I kiss your hand which is interlocked with mine as I'm
   driving;
It's my favourite thing.
One eye is on you, the other on the road, with no real
   destination
Because where I want to be is next to you.

Let's get lost.
Nowhere is too far when home sits in the passenger seat.
I wanna stop and take photos of every "big" thing each small
   town has to offer on the roadside.

Let's make memories.
The only thing I want to carry is your hand in mine,
A bag on my back of funny stories
And a lifetime of good choices.

Capacity

Sit in it.
Yeah, that's what I said.
Sit in those uncomfortable feelings even for a small second
　　long enough to let it sink in.
Take it all on board, you have the room.

What a waste, to have the capacity but not the will,
To feel as strongly as we can, the good, the sad, and the
　　despair.
Some call it torture;
Poets call it art.

Rhiannon

Tough love can be a real bitch,
It comes in the form of a friend
With a smile and a soft hand,
It's not what you want to hear,
It's what needs to be said,

She was a first 'real friend',
A chaotic mess drenched in stress,
I wouldn't have her any other way,

I remember adventures together,
Fighting in the car over which plan was better,
She's unconditional, comfortable and kind,
There's so much love in the hazel of her eyes.

Can I ask?

Would it be okay
If all I wanted in life, was you?
Sure, I have ambitions, but I've known and believed in myself
   long enough to know,
Those things will happen if I work for them.
I don't need you like air,
I need you like when you miss an old friend,
Or when you haven't spoken with your mother in a while.
I need you like I need a video call with my best friend.
Perhaps I need you to rest after a long flight.
You're a need in a way that adds comfort,
A healthy addition to a life I know is worth living either way.

Sliding Doors

When the evening came, summer started packing its things.
You stood swaying in the hallway,
And that's when I found you,
In the sliding door moment.

Two souls locked eyes and you took a seat.
Something just aligned that night,
Like Achilles and Patroclus,
Two people on the earth stood before one another.
And for a moment,
Or a lifetime,
All they saw was each other.

Dear CJ

Give me back my
             Words,
 They were my
             First treasure.

Betrayal

The feeling of betrayal is like the tear of a muscle.
The feelings that didn't matter,
And if I didn't hurt you, what made me easy prey?
Where there are wounds and scars,
You see targets marked.

My kindness was a weakness,
I could give you what you needed for a moment or two.
But brief lies and blurred lines painted our course.
The lies flicked from your tongue like a sting,
Like wasps when fruit of known truths grow on observant
    leaves
Come hovering to take its sweet juices.
The apple doesn't fall far from the poisoned tree.

Belong Here

I hope that when you wake up in the morning,
And make your cold brew coffee
That you think of me.
I hope that when warm light graces your soft light skin,
That those feelings wrap around you like my arms do,
Like when butterflies see skies,
And our lips meet.

Let's eat and go out and play.
Let's awkwardly dance to a song we love because no one
    around cares more than us.
Come along to *my* plans, friends of friends,
You're stamped with my ink on our package deal.

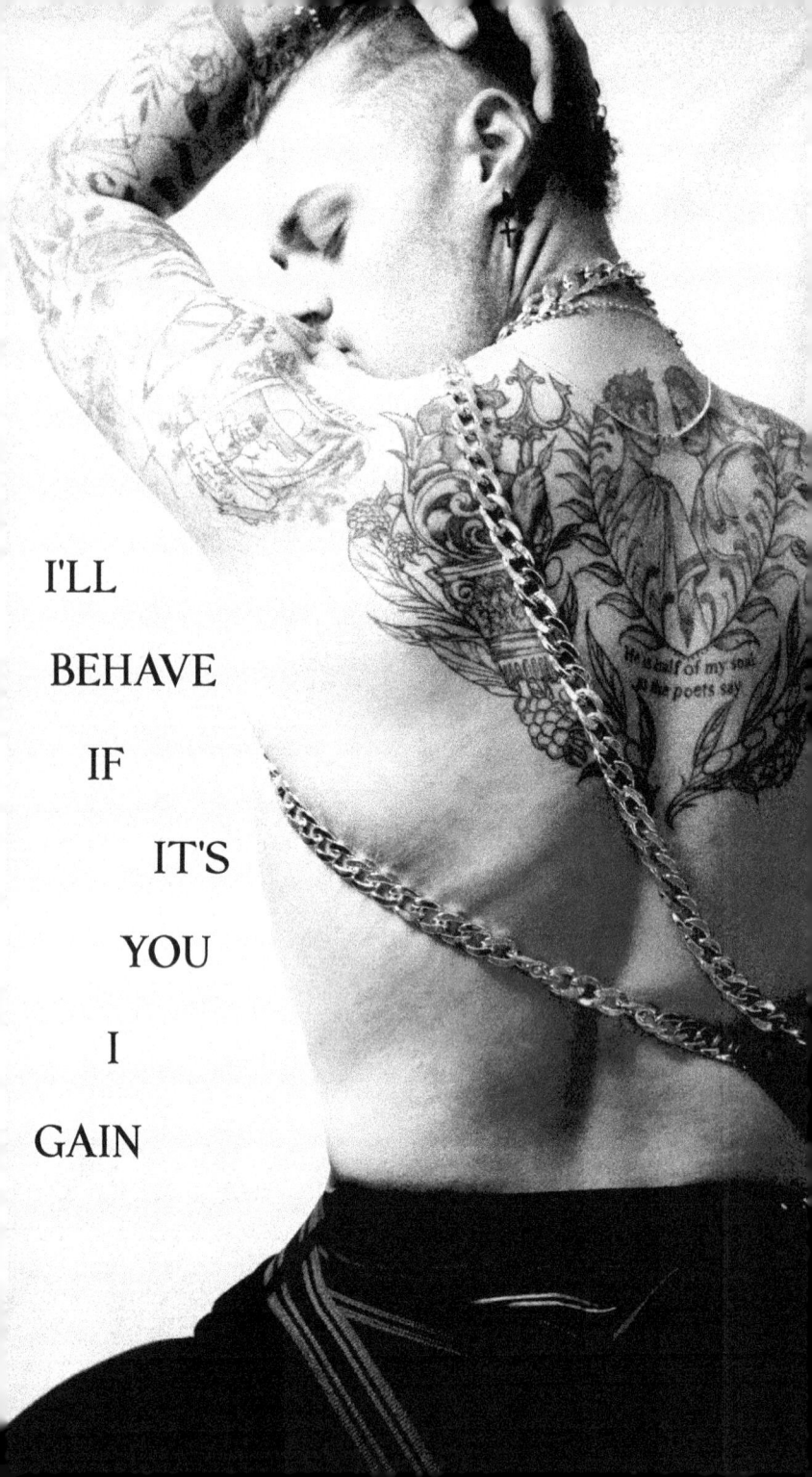

I'LL

BEHAVE

IF

IT'S

YOU

I

GAIN

The Pub

Small fights, chilly nights, pub nights,
Drinks flow, no coat,
Hair is overgrown.

I'd come home, with no hope, but drink alone.
Lights on, TV spits sound, no one around.

I called, "Hey, come by."
You arrived.
Let's call it a night.

Now it's pub crawls, dinner hall and we're having a ball.

Now it's my place, your place, *our* place.

Boyfriend Stuff

When I say I want to be with you, I don't just mean the
    boyfriend stuff.
I want to be with you at home for moments of peace after a
    long day,
To feel cosy on movie nights.
Or with you for awkward family dinners
Because your sister and her mister still haven't forgiven you
    for last year's Christmas.
Or maybe being alongside you when you stumble on your
    words and don't know what to say,
My hand will firmly grip your knee to put you at ease.

Isn't it a pretty thought, to think we would have each other
    going round for round at the bar? Let's clink drinks and say
    cheers.
Although days and moments pass by, let's make it years.
So, when we're old and frail and lines run like rivers on our
    faces,
I will smile because of a life well spent.

I want to be with you for the long drive home,
Because car rides feel like sunrises when we're all alone.
I'd like to think I could be with you on special days,
The kind where we pray for no rain, like birthdays, holidays,
    and Christmas Day.
We can figure it out as we go, there's no rush or pressure
    here.
Just us taking it easy,
In good company.

A Gentle Reminder

In this moment,
At this place,
I am safe.

All of the Boys

You placed your hands on my skin and kissed my lips,
That's when I knew I wanted you, the whole of you.
You shared stories from your past and I learned who you
    were,
And who you are.
I learned that I love you for all of you;
Your mistakes,
Heartbreaks,
And missed chances.

All of the boys who have had you before created dead-end
    roads,
Blurred lines in mapped heartbeats and casual letdowns.
To them, I say thank you.
It is them too that I am grateful for,
Because I know I can love you more.

Model Materiel

There's nobody like you,
Nothing stands in your way,
I could sculpt a man of model clay,
And every inch of his muscle I'd trace,
I'd bite my lips and press my fingers into the lines of your
	face,
I am fixated on the design of you,
Nothing will ever undo the labour of love and obsession.

Just Kiss Me Again

We met and moved fast,
One night under the stars and you're in my arms,
One week apart and we met at the parade park.
Take it from there, there's no trips or snares,
We will kiss in the dark, till we meet again.

Fast forward a fortnight, and I want you to be mine
But unspoken words trembled up the stairs,
Laying naked bare, I ask about what we are.
Thoughts cast a line in my mind,
Poets think like this all the time.

Days

34 days and mine and yours were all the same.
29 days and your sunshine awoke butterflies like spring dew
    days.
7 days and you walked me to the train, same clothes from the
    parade,
6 days and we dance in a bar with my hands in your hair,
"I'm so glad you're here" is whispered in my ear.

One night we passed in a hallway,
Who could have thought that these days just rolled together
As naturally as ocean waves?

The String

Do you believe in an invisible string?
The
    Tug
        Tug
            Tug
I felt to sit where I sat, on the night we met,
 The thread left flaring from your pocket,
So my room key was the only solution.
What about the string that walked you home lonely?
So, when one day we met, you found a home in me.

Let's talk about the cast line that left doubts in my mind
   about motives and intentions.
It's the same thread that led to nights in your bed,
Wondering how I could be so lucky.

The Bridges We Do Not See

Let's build a bridge with no design or plan.
Will we ever cross it?
That will never matter.
What's on the other side?
Let's make it up, either good, bad or irrationally ugly.
But why?
Start building till I tell you to stop.
But my breaths are sharp and heavy,
I don't know where to start.
Breathing is tight.
Panic.
Keep going, let your mind just run.
Stop.

I permit myself to come back to the moment in the here and
    now.

San Clemente

I've always wondered about the San Clemente Syndrome.
Layers upon layers of history built upon one another,
Memory-mapped tunnels in between,
Connecting every part of ourselves at one point or another.
We have layers of ourselves that we can show people and take
    through tours.
Knowing someone in that kind of way is more than one
    dimension.

I think of how histories cannot be relived, just reflected on.
I have no control over our past.
So, I will go through the paths you show me and admire the
    scenery,
Taking it all in piece by piece
As I reconcile this history long after the tour is over.

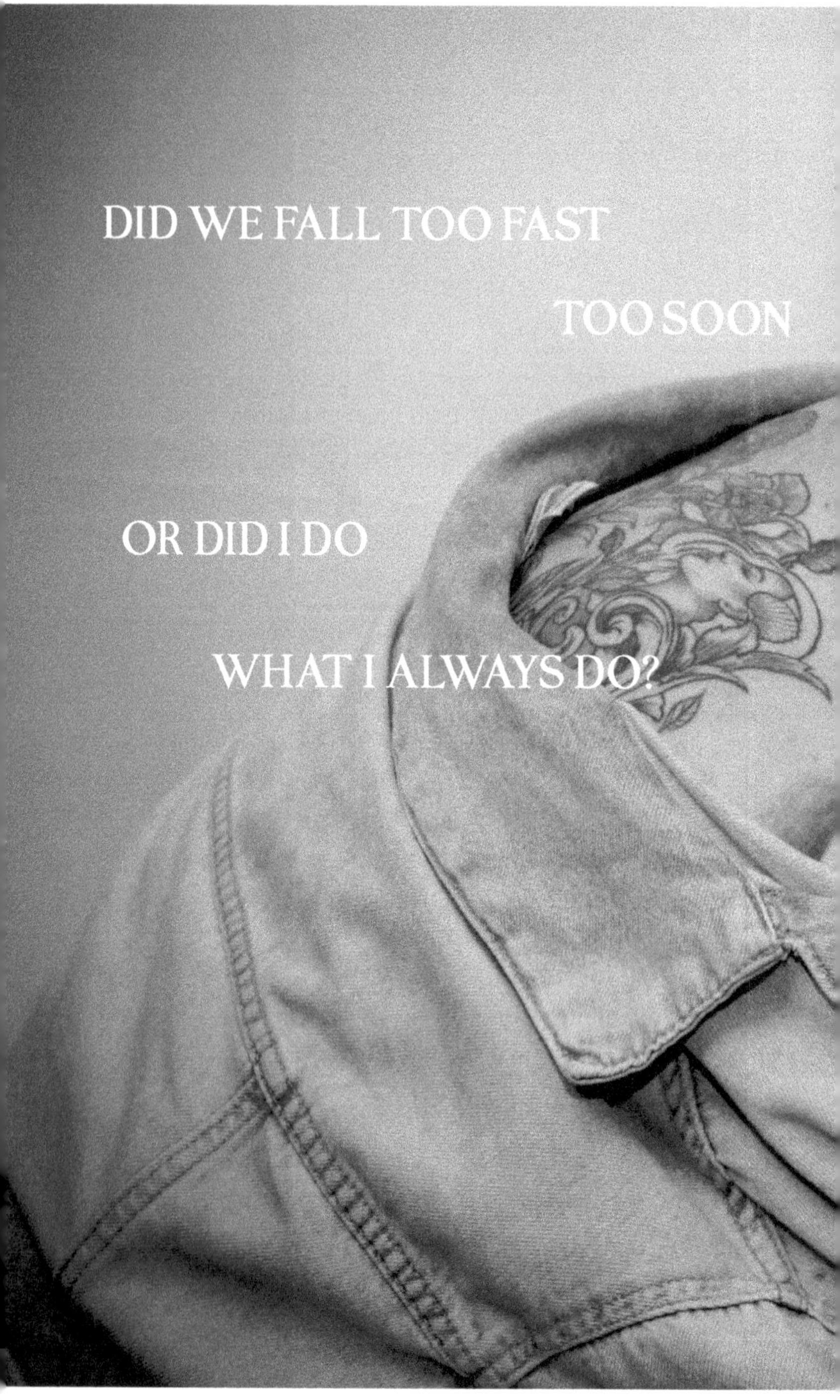
DID WE FALL TOO FAST
TOO SOON
OR DID I DO
WHAT I ALWAYS DO?

Mum

Dear Mum,
You were just trying your best, in the way you could.
And that's okay.
I feel your love every day.
In every way.

2 am

It's 2 am and the dinner drinks have turned into giggles
There are conversations over an outdoor table on my friend's
    back porch.
Those cherished moments of laughter made me think of you,
Because when I share beautiful little moments,
I want you to have them too, gift-wrapped in my finest
    layers.
We pour another glass and share a burst of laughter.
I saved you a seat
Where you should be.
 The moment captures me,
And suddenly,
I grasp the chair next to me.

Just Friends

If "just being friends" were a solar system, I'd give anything to
    be in your orbit,
I'd aim for the moon in hopes of reaching your stars,
But in the end, your gravity would pull me off guard.
So, now I settle for Pluto.

Dear Nepo Baby

You remind me of fresh coffee, the kind that stains my teeth.
You're the exciting dip at ocean baths on the first day of
    summer, the salt that burns my skin.
You're the cigarette between my lips, the first drag that soaks
    my lungs like sponges.
You're the biggest regret of all, the chances never taken, car
    ridden with words left unsaid,
Alone in empty cities, all my thoughts are misread.

City Secrets

If cities could talk, they would tell me to move on.
Because the one who was never mine is one who's not lost,
I watch cars driven backward and forwards,
The rat race around town, lost in lights I walk.

This city is supposed to be romantic, isn't it?
No.
Then why am I sitting in the hotel lobby with less heart to
    give than yesterday?
Why is Christmas Eve suddenly the hardest day of the year?
Perhaps what I saw was my own story becoming spilled ink
    on the poet's page,
Making way for city walls to tell the story of his city, his story
    in his way.

That Summer

It was a summer breeze that smacked me hard in the face,
First day off the plane.
Loving you didn't ruin my life.
Sweltering summer days still burn,
Not on the skin, but somewhere deeper.
It's the evening panic when I have no plans,
But the lost souls that walk between walls of cityscapes.
That meant something to me.
You meant something to me.
But radio silence still sends signals all the same.

Back in Australia

I hate the way you jester, like you've got a secret to tell,
I hate the way you smile, I know it's all for show,
I hate that I never know what you're thinking,
I wish I could read your mind,
Because for you, it all looks so easy, leaving me behind.

New York Fucking City

Legs walk over sidewalks, history draped in stone and
    cement,
For years
I'd try and gather it.
The words that are, tell you my piece of picked pocket mind,
Something was stolen from me,
No.
The city has its charm, and knows how to use it well;
Once something is uncovered, you're in the old wives' group
    who bear its own.
You are the man caught purple-handed,
And cold-blooded lifeless hands jingling with Tommy's
    watch.
Times Square wouldn't know what hit it.
A devilish smile looks much like an angel,
Until you see wings and horns all start the same.

Touch Down

Sometimes when a plane touches down in LA,
It isn't the jittery excitement that keeps me up all night.
It's the low dim lights, pictures snapped of moments passing
   by.
It's the memory of you that I already know will be faint,
Because winter snow isn't always an excuse to keep warm.

High End

We made it to the city, where I wished you kissed me,
We made it to Room 40, you're my story,
We made it to the desert, and that's where it hurts.
Yes, right there,
You put the end in the "high end."

EVEN FOR A NIGHT

JUST TAKE

MY HEART

AND

SHOW ME

MY WORLD

ONCE

MORE

Unlearned Behaviours

I can gaze at the tea leaves and together we can mastermind
   the ending.
I can pluck people's feelings like pillow feathers;
Maybe I could write you a love letter?
I can twist tales and tables, stilt skin tricks in my cabinet of
   dreams,
It's a wondrous thing, isn't it?
For years I thought I could manage it-
The nasty taste of salt-brimmed peach Bellini breakfast cups,
The sharpness of a tongue, concealed through handsome
   smiles, lures them in,
Until one smile too far, one tale told too fatuously, one hair
   out of place,
 And my silver snare glimmers a moment too long.

Your City

Your city is a handsome dreamscape
Every twenty-something once fantasised of.
It is the bright skyline and sunset drenched in golden hours;
For years I'd dreamt of it.

Your city is a home-built garden in brick apartments.
Spare a penny for seeds to water it.
Rain doesn't fall as generously as it used to.

Your city is a dimly lit bar where a boy wearing a white gold
    ring offers you a drink,
A slip of the tongue perhaps?
He's the devil's child managing his taxes on an after-hours'
    nightcap.

Your city is the message left unread, the words left unsaid,
And the final phrase that would keep me up in my bed.
A hotel lobby appears in my imagination,
"Go," I hear my own whisper.
A quick trip downstairs and a packed luggage bag later;
He sits and waits while flinching through final goodbyes.

Your city is a smoke bomb of unclear friendly hands,
Fingers deep in my peach-skin collarbone,
Is it a slip or a trick?
Experiment with me until you're sure the colours don't sit
    right on your clean skin,
Revisit in the morning to strip me with words over half-
    hearted messages.
Rinse and repeat it.
Do it all again.

Your city is a lie, a fractured moment in time,
One that was never mine.

26/2/24

I still have his scent all over me, the musk of a lost Sunday
  evening in a small room.
Just us two,
Back from overseas and all I had was me,
Now he's all I see.

His head nestled into my chest, sleeping soundly,
Like when you let your head fall into capable arms, there is a
  sense of security there.
He's safe with me, and I with him.
He turns to me, still half asleep,
"I don't want to go" I utter as my heart is filled with the fruits
  of someone new.
He chuckles, eyes still heavy as sunlight's orange glow fills
  Sydney streets
"Then don't," he replied.

Tell Me I'm Wrong

Maybe, just maybe,
There was an open door,
A slightly longer touch,
A missed cab ride home,
A seat in the lobby,
A key to room 40,
A map of the places we'd never been,
And maybe, just maybe,
I made it mean more than it did.

AS

The colours of your clothes always clash,
The smile on your face lines your moustache,
The cold brew coffee you sip,
On a sleepy Saturday morning trip,

You're a man of few words,
No coherent way of explaining,
So, I will always need your voice to feel safe and heard;
To move my heart, and give me momentum.

And now because of you,
I drink cold brew,
And now when colours clash,
I think they're beautiful too.

.

Hometown

On my first trip to your hometown,
The scenery, made up of all the spots that raised you,
Some were difficult to see, like where you hooked up with
    him.

But when we kissed in your bedroom, it was like striking
    matches;
All my old habits,
Came burning down, ashes to ashes.
Your hands on me just felt so right,
But I have a hometown too, memories made, and the
    moments that raised me.
Maybe curiosity is a one-sided street,
Or maybe flowers bloom on both sides
And only one of us dares to pick its petals.

You by My Side

While you slept beside me,
There were a couple of visits and exchanged words;
I started to feel it, the end of all the endings.

Your back stretched across my line of sight,
Breath rising and falling in safety and comfort,
Fuck, the things I'd do to keep you safe just like this.

You grabbed my hand and pulled it around your body,
My caramel skin cradled your body.
It was a firm embrace;
I traced my fingers over your body and spelt those letters.

I gave any reason to not trust you,
Far too cynical to believe you just wanted me for me,
But the glass pearls of safety, I kept close to my chest.
To this day they are still safe and unscratched.

Then I knew them, those smiles,
Your friends,
My friends,
And the loose ends,
Time mends.

I spelt out letters that tickle your skin,
You giggled curiously and my lips were sealed,
But now I'm ready to tell you,
Love of my life.

Opposite Attraction

That hair pushed back,
I prefer the colour black,
Yet your style,
Your body wrapped in colour,
Makes me want you forever.

My hair is curly and in my eyes,
Your hair stands like brunette spikes,
I know words between the pages of books,
You know local bands and drink cans.

I'm Tired

You and I don't sleep the same way.
While your peace and clear-headed mental spaces guide you
    to have smooth, slow sleep,
I lay awake, predicting events that may never actually
    happen.
It's starting to occur to me that people talk about me far
    more than
I imagined, in ways both kind and cruel.

Aching Bellies

There is nothing more genuine and beautiful in this world
Than holding aching bellies from laughter with friends,
When bad problems lay flat on cloudy beds where I place my
    head,
And rest.
Their company saves me in ways they might never see or
    understand,
And there's beauty in finding creatively kind ways of saying
    thanks.

IT TOOK

ONLY

THREE DAYS

TO

GIVE

YOURSELF

AWAY

PART 2

BAD HABITS

The Breakup Text

██

I just had to think some things through to be sure, ████████

████████████████ I wanna be completely honest ████████

███

████████, you're a █████████ person ███ I love. ███████

███

███████████████████████████████ I █████████

███

████████ see ███████████ the future, ████████ I don't

wanna hurt you████████████████████████ I don't

wanna stop hanging ████ you █████████████████████

████████████████████████████ don't █████

████ think ████ you've done something wrong ████████

███████████ you've been an amazing person, ██████████

███████████████████████████████████████

████████████████████████████████ a relation-

ship is what I wanted █████████ I wanted one with you ████

███

███

████████ I just feel so sorry for laying this on you ███████ I

know this will be hard, █████████████████████████

████████████████ I'm sorry ████████████████████

███

████████████████████████████

Morning of Heartbreak

Clichés thrown across the table,
Small remarks and half-assed advice from those who don't
    think twice,
They say that ways these days are different,
And "darling it's just harder in this generation."
Never seen,
Behind screens,
Mum and Dad search for consoling words,
They tell me I'll be fine,
But something is dead inside me.
So the vapour fills my lungs like wells of water,
Nicotine hits my head like blows to the face,
For a moment over breakfast, I get to be numb from the pain
    of past days.

Bad Choices

My bad choices follow me,
Like locks of cut hair, found days after the choice was made.
They are like the 3 am ravens that crow by my bedside,
The body under my bed,
And the skeleton in my closet.
They are the all-consuming thoughts that drive me to the
    edge,
Until suddenly solemn screams halt the screeching
And then breathing feels easy.

Along for the Ride

You dragged me along for the ride, and for every cut.
The bruise I wore is like a badge of honour,
The prize for my patience and kindness,
Showered in bloody kisses.
Love is pain and a sting.
My jewel, my pride,
I, for the first time,
Think I'll never be alright.
The love of my life is lost in a time
Of broken dreams,
And friendly fire.
I called one more time
Because who am I if I go down without a fight?
This doesn't come easily,
I have to get up and try,
I know better than to give up on hard days,
But you had different plans anyway,
Led me to paradise only to befriend me,
As if we ever were,
I paint on my best smile,
Cracking at either side,
Utter that vile label,
No choice or power,

We are just friends.

Grand Southern

Our heavy limbs and eyes draped over one another in the
    hotel room.
We joked with each other between breaths,
We giggled and locked eyes.
Then in the middle of the night, before the sun's early rising,
Those three words left your lips,
And all at once.
My heart beats,
Not like this,
But ever since.

The Boy Who Broke
the Poet's Heart

I just wonder and wonder,
What it ever meant,
To the boy who broke the poet's heart.
Fuck it, I've come so far,
And what's past is past,
But only sorrowful red flags fly at half-mast.

The small tokens of love beyond our years,
Somehow overlooked amid your own fears,
For a moment I was his and he was mine,
But the tables turned,
Crimson flags ignored,
I'm colour blind.

What about the August bracelet I wore every day?
It brought me only good things, like you,
Or think about how I made you my whole damn world,
Only for you to set sights on any other man's eyes.
Let's talk about how it only took you three fucking days to
    give yourself away.
You're sinister and twisted if you don't think that would hurt
In the cracks between smiles of your indifference,
Pain blooms, twisting like ivy around the heart's fragile tendrils.

My head can't swim past lost evenings in tiny beds next to
    you,
Falling for you when the night ends,
And trusting you like my best friend.
How do you save the world when your world ends?

I didn't want to leave but how the hell could I stay, if this is
    our fate anyway?
How can I be just a friend, and watch another man take you
    to bed?
You want the best for me but never mind;
It's a humbug way to say goodbye when nothing's healed.

You told me you hope I find someone who loves me the way
    I deserve,
But those sentiments only make those wounds worse,
Because my whole life changed in a moment, and here I am
    left to pick up the pieces.
I'm still doing time for that crime.
Dazzling disaster, I try to remind myself, "I'm fine"
But I can't keep it together when you're not mine.

Peace

I like to think that one day,
There comes a moment when you come up,
A memory, photo, or even funny story,
Perhaps even running into you,
And I don't feel numb, or I don't feel hurt or rage.
I just feel at peace with what I feel.
I just like to think that you're somewhere laughing,
Having a drink like I know you love to do,
And we're both doing okay.

One Day I'll Be Alright

People will always tell you that blocking him is easier,
Or that no contact will make the pain move quicker,
But what stops me from cutting him from me, is knowing he
   was part of me too,
I know me well enough to know that burning down our
   house of memories
Comes with collateral damage I can't undo,
He might be fine, but I'd fade to ashes too.

One of these days I'll wake up and it won't sting like a cut
   from kitchen knives,
Too close to the hand I sliced,
I catch myself thinking, *what if he's once in a lifetime?*
Not everyone gets this chance,
And the man who they cannot stand, was part of my future
   plans.

The No -Contact Phase

Some moments I catch myself thinking about you for no
    good reason,
Like when a song by The Gorillaz starts to play,
Or when cold brew coffee becomes my drink of choice even
    when it rains,
I didn't stop to think how you gave me a glimpse of the
    whole world,
But what's a world without you walking beside me?
What signs did I not see?
Did you leave clues between couch cushions and messages
    between pillow kisses?
Some things just don't have an answer, and it's answers I
    think I need.

You popped up on my phone screen,
"Long time no see"
How have you been?
That smile graces my eyes and kisses my tender wounds
    tight,
It's the same boy I know I loved,
But you're not my "someone" I'm seeing,

Your good intentions are arson to my own wellbeing,
You just want to be friends in times when I'm not playing
    pretend,
I'm not here to waste time,
Here with you is where I saw my life,
I wanted to sightsee,
Be your eye candy,
How the fuck do I move on when the block button moves
    beyond the seven seas?
Somewhere I refuse to see, in places I cannot meet,
I can't have you.
But I do have me.

What Highschool English Taught Me

They say to write what you know,
Those experiences that follow you wherever you go,
Tales told over time,
Experiences of mine, the story went untold.

My teacher told me that we cannot choose where we start off
 in life,
But we can choose where we go from there,
Everything since that day in the classroom,
I have put pen to paper, as she told me to do,

I write about the boy who loved a drink, a weekend away and
 for a moment, me.
The same boy who let me breathe in the nicotine of his
 kisses.
I write about the chance encounter that flipped my world,
And the day at the parade where we learned feelings were the
 same,

He who held my hand and made me feel *safe*,
For him, I'd die for his many sins,
Yet here I pay in seething pain,
And here he sits in the same old town,
The same beige, plain lounge,
Sipping the same cheap drinks,
Talking with the same two friends,
Yet not a memory of me.

FOREVER

HAUNTED BY

THE WHAT IFS

AND

IF ONLYS

youcan'ttakeitback

Soft hair, smoke flares,
I'll pretend you're just not for me,
But we both know, darling,
All your friends said I'm perfect.
If it's not me,
How can I compete?
I'll go to your hometown,
Dance around your best friend's house
Like I bought the whole block,
And you never found out I was even around,
That weekend.

I only came to this shitty town,
In hopes that you'd reach out,
And I'm excited now,
Enjoying myself anyhow,
You're gonna see me in their stories,
And wonder why you left me,
But you can't take it back.

Without You

The hardest part about parting ways and letting go isn't in
  what you said to me,
The hardest part is feeling you slip away from me,
My memories becoming features
And in between every cherished moment I share with my
  friends there's a joke or a song
That reminds me of you,
And now I sit here pondering the thought,
Knowing one day you'll move on too,
Life's hardest lesson is learning to live without you.

For our vices we pay prices,
But for you I pay twice as much as the masses,
For I cannot come to terms with the lessons I've learned,
I'm scared.
Because one day you might remember me too and perhaps be
  too scared to reach out.

Even if you do,
What would we say?

He Who Runs Scared

I'll never forget the night you said you loved me,
Wound around in hotel bedsheets,
The same city where you met me,
We played cards and exchanged hearts,
I watched as the man who ran scared burnt down our house
    of cards,
You held the light,
But I had the matches stashed away in my pocket,
I asked for your hand, and you almost forgot it.

Two days and we passed away,
Not a word or a breath for 48 hours and I reach out,
Work has you down, we're over now,
But can I ask?

Were you ever someone,
Who wanted me in the end?
How did you love me then leave me on read?
Were you ever thinking when you told me "we're fine"?
You couldn't give me an answer and I gave you the time,
You held my hand at parties and touched my thigh,
You always had the upper hand when I gave you mine,
Will you one day give me answers for saying goodbye?
Let's not pretend you didn't do it,
You're the one who blew it,
The man who ran scared because he was committed.

26th of February

The day we met floods my brain like the shitty wine I drink
To forget every part of me you touched through a silhouette
   of sunshine on that fateful day,
But I purge the sour taste,
The feeling of never quite knowing where we went wrong,
You'll tell me you don't know,
Neither do I babe,
I reflect looking backwards,
Hoping that somewhere I went wrong,
At least then I'd know *I'm the one to blame babe,*
You're all I wanted in every shape and way I could conjure,
I am forever afflicted by the way you wonder,
Never knowing your story,
"I wish things were different" you say,
You and me both, babe.

One Phone Call

The hardest thing I've ever had to do,
Was put in place a barrier between me and you,
Come to my country music town,
I'm not sure if your presence would make or break me,
But patience and time to heal holes left from sleeping by
  your loveless side,
I would reach out to touch you knowing it isn't what you
  wanted,
I built my life around the castles you crumbled,
Like an actor at a show,
I look for my lines in the dress rehearsal,
But it's not my role in this lifetime,
When will you just say goodbye?

1999

What I feel from you is cold,
I made it something more,
You're twenty-something years old and still won't pick up
  your phone,
Moments without you creep up quickly,
A pair of mindless messes making way through their
  twenties,
I shared my life and in poems and stories,
My hand reaches for the book, and you ask for the summary,
No one gets to me more than you can,
Age is fast and twenty-five leaves me wondering what time I
  lost,
You standby as we pass time and progress seems far,
Still stuck where you are,
And I'm broken in the same parts.

66 Days

In what we thought could be a lifetime,
The world changed,
In 66 days we breezed by like a summer haze,
And in the talking phase,
We paved our own way.
My eyes met your gaze,
And I knew things would never be the same,
Because in 66 days you showed me what love felt like on my
    bare skin,
As natural as sin,
I wanna touch touch touch you again.

Your imprint on my heart left a mark,
If I could go back to the start,
In that hallway you passed,
I would stop you and live it all again,
Because for 66 days I had the love of my life,
And countless days will pass,
But your touch jumpstarted the beat in my heart,
And made all the difference.

My Place, Your Place, Bar, Coffee Shop

The clichés they say are true for a reason,
The man who only loved me for a season,
April blues come too soon,
But by May I had fucking hell to pay,
Two days and he fades into shades of grey,
Then there's that text because you didn't have the nerve to
    say it to my face,
So I sit here in my room reserved for you,
Only to find out he who I claimed as "mine"
Slides into the messages of some other guy,
It took him days to move on but for me it takes time,
He revives his bachelor photos in search of "friends and fun
    for now",
It's not him trapped in his own mental cages searching for a
    way out,
And I'll write about him in my craft,
Pictures of him I'd burn because some heart's been lost,
Isn't it insensitive to drink the way you drank,
To call me when I'm driving home and confess you miss
    some parts of me,

The pain from remembering your text is all that's left,
But between bruises and my poem pages you twisted knives
    in my gut,
At least I am a dear good friend,
Some kind of award just for showing up.

It's Been Real, Sydney

I had looked forward to that weekend for a while; my days were encased with thoughts of everything we would get to do and every sight there was to see. My plan was to spoil you, because nobody does selfless, nice things. I wanted you to feel special, like when we twisted in hotel sheets, and you said you loved me. What a fucking legacy to leave your lips and make *me* feel like this world was built for just us two. Those days came to an end as they do, the weekend faded, and all seemed fine. Your eyes held distance as we watched the city skyline. But like life has it, I look backwards in hoping to move *forwards*. I cannot help but wish I did something differently. If only I knew it was the last time.

I wish I squeezed your hand just a little tighter that Sunday morning. I wish I looked at you a few seconds longer just to watch you smile one more time. I wish I ran my fingers through your hair, and pressed my fingers on your thigh where I wrote a note that's inked in black. You were mine. I wish I had pointed out how beautiful the sky looked that morning before the gloom came over my aeroplane window.

When I touched down in my hometown, part of me wanted to turn around and tell you I loved you one last time. But as I look back you said goodbye from more than 427 kilometres away. I was idiotic to think that you'd tell me we'd be fine. So, when I see Sydney lights, I die inside. Those streets are flooded with your breaths on my neck and your legs between my sheets. Losing you was losing me. I'll stop and search for those little pieces of everything that came before you. My blue skies don't shine like the sunrise. It's all just shattered pieces of me wishing for more time.

I Don't Sleep the Same

I don't sleep how I used to,
It's a truth I sit with when my eyes tighten and I
                                        Try
                                            Try
                                                Try
To drift into a lonesome sleep,
But it's me who I live with, in each wink,
Me without you is as unnatural to me as not closing my eyes
    to laugh,
I feel the distance in my bed,
And wonder where you are instead,
The streetlight that looms in my room,
Casts a light on the side of the bed left for you.

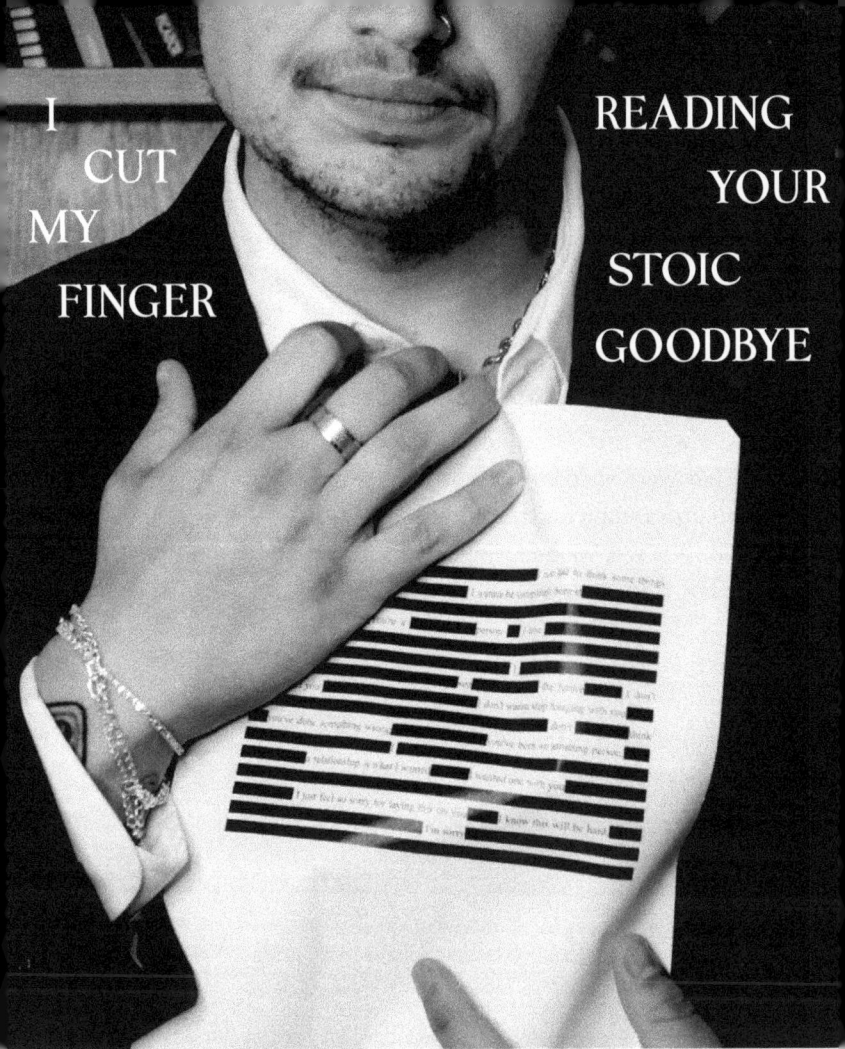

I
CUT
MY
FINGER

READING

YOUR

STOIC

GOODBYE

Green Eyes

I've never met someone unrelated to me with green eyes,
They were once my most striking feature,
So uncommon and uncanny,
Like the way we met,
A boy from a movie.

Your eyes give me a glimpse into your whole world,
And for a moment I was so lost,
I pulled out a map,
Took your hand,
And said *let's look together.*

Fuck It

I had so many hopes for us,
And when I write this here in my home,
Too many beers to see clear but I mean it,
Oh boy do I mean it.

I hoped that one day you would move off that same lounge
    you drank your life away but it's true,
You'd take your eyes off your phone when you had my eyes to
    look into,
Maybe you didn't walk away and say we're through,
You could have said we moved too fast too soon,
But here I am stuck in the walls of my bedroom,
Unable to move,
Fuck you and fuck love because my feelings are valuable too.

Not a single uncircumspect breath was spent on asking how
    I felt,
No questions or coaxing me for my hot take,
Just a snow globe heart that you shook to watch it break,
Don't shed tears when your biggest fears led us here.
Now I dread getting out of bed,
Because every time-stamped moment of you is laced in
    everything I do.
My feelings clearly misled.

My Compass Still Points to You

I sit behind the wheel after a night with friends,
That's always how my new nights end,
The front of my house is a strange place now,
Knowing somewhere out there you're sinking drinks in the
    cushions of your couch,
Out west, the boy I gave my best to is just a transient being
    somehow,
Our love was like a compass,
Pointing only to you,
But somehow along the way you forgot its importance,
To pull me home and give me purpose.

Holidays

Holidays pass me by like numbers
On a calendar crossed off with black markers
Ink on the pages growing every day I don't see you,
So tell me what's the difference
Between Halloween and Christmas?
All it means is distance
If it's another celebration without your presence,
I'm isolated from that heart throbbing sensation
Of your kiss leaving me breathless.

Committed

Perhaps the reason you left me stranded is because of what
   they all said,
The casual commentary across the table.
They said "he's perfect for you"
"He could make you happy"
"He has it all figured out"
You two were meant to meet,
And meant to be.
Like the pieces of a puzzle you fit into my hand effortlessly,
I was so sure of you,
And that was the scariest thing of all,
Because once you're in the haze of good days,
And I become your special place
Then there's everything to lose.

I Drink Too Much

I think I've picked up the habit of drinking too much,
I catch you crawling up in my brain when I'm around the
warm table of friends,
Trying my best to forget the nights with you I wished would
never end,
I sink drinks that taste sweet in hopes of forgetting the place
you said we'd meet,
But perceived romance and emo bands became cancelled
plans,
So I'll take a drink and pretend it doesn't sting.
In fact, I'll finish the whole damn bottle as my friends help
me from the table,
It's a habit I gotta kick, loving you drove me to the end of the
bottle,
But I think I'll stay here.

Caffeine, nicotine,
Anything to release the dopamine,
It all rushed to my head,
Nothing beats the chemicals that are released when you're in
my bed
Next to me,
Now I'm an addict knowing that'll never be.

Addictive Personality

Is it possible to be longing for a smile?
Not just any smile but *his* smile,
And the intoxicating smell of his body on my pillow,
The drinks taste smooth when clinking them with him,
Down too easy.

Like any good addict I will take any measure to orchestrate
    an encounter,
Or to find ourselves alone with time to kill,
Just to get my fix of situational thrill,

I'd trade any good money for his car to break down
So I could drive him home and be his saviour,
My skin itches for him to scratch the surface of my need for
    him shirtless,
Pressed against my skin and so full of sin,
I get drunk on the lust as the bedposts thrust,
Hands down my back and raised red lines like I've been
    attacked.

Let me drive you fucking crazy,
So when I'm gone, you crave me.

Holding It for a Friend

One kiss
> And

A   huff
> > Of smoke
> > > > Was all
> > > it took

And I knew I'd be hooked.

Stoic Goodbye

Ever wanted to scream but you couldn't?
Have you felt so winded you couldn't even force it?
I'll write it here,
Just in case I can't bring myself to ignore him,
Fuck you for the hell you put me through
Only to safeguard yourself,
Those shallow words fade into nothing when you can't
    absorb them,
My pain from the damage you left isn't even on the radar,
It's more like a birthmark,
Evidence that you've been here the whole time.

Folklore tells me it's a wound from a past life,
The patch of skin where you burned the knife,
Only yours wasn't sharp and pointed,
It was a stoic goodbye I cut my fingers on reading every time.

Move Past It

Your friends reach out with all the faith and confidence in
   the world,
"You'll be fine, I see your strength" they say,
Then why can't I move past it,
Press delete and pretend you were never a thing for me?

It's been just over a fortnight,
The one thing I can't buy is time.
I can't figure things out,
Nor do I want to.
I think I'll just sit in it for a few moments more,
The days roll into weeks and all at once,
I feel you slipping from me like a distant memory,
Don't say it's fine,
It takes time,
You seek distance but to your town, I'll drive.

PART 3

NEW HABITS

I Just Want to Heal

The morning routine repeats itself,
Move your body and drink your water,
"You'll feel better," they say,
Take your drive and do your job,
It'll keep you focused.
Work on your craft,
Make clever remarks,
But from a broken heart
Comes a new start.

A World of Firsts

In a world of firsts, I've never experienced anything like this.
You were the first of so many painted portraits of happy
     couples in love,
The first time I've ever loved this deeply,
Like when you press your fingers into a peach and bruise the
     skin,
I lay awake with every indent of you all over me.

You were the first person I knew I loved instinctively,
It felt more natural than breathing,
To breathe in the smoke from our flames brought by fate,
Intoxicating.
I will always picture you laughing and smiling,
Because you were here,
And you happened,
That's empirical evidence that I enter into my memory box,
Forever reminding me that the day we met
Changed my whole world.

Let Go

Letting someone go isn't as straightforward as they say,
Nor is it a single decision made in the clearest light of day.
It's a process of letting go of those small pieces that made
    them part of you,
And that hurts in ways nobody can imagine
Until its 2 am and you're sitting in it.

It's the changes in routine,
And the departure of everything you've gotten used to
All at once,
Take time, they say,
Easier said in a moment's breath then lived through every
    day,
But healing will come when you trust,
One day, maybe not today
Or tomorrow,
But you will be okay.

257 Kilometres Away

Distance is more than just missed messages,
Or just roads between homes,
It's the faint-hearted exchanges,
Two hundred and fifty-seven kilometres separate us two,
Two hundred and fifty-seven reasons why I can't stop loving
    you.

I'd walk those railway lines passing minimal streetlights.
Even if it meant a moment more of your time,
But I cannot look past,
The levels of incomplete sentences and

                                            watered
                                                down
                                                    words
Of best wishes,
Pour them into my mouth,
For more I'd drown.

An Innocent Visit

I bit the bullet,
I drank the juice,
Got in my car
And drove to you.
Your hometown seems so distant now.

Last time I took this drive,
Was so we could spend some time,
But now it's just to see friends.
Highways bend and stretch
I swear this road never ends.

The stars shine differently out here,
I pictured a life where you were near,
Not a man in a mullet handing me a visitor's card,
Who says he can't stay long.

Things Don't Feel Over

Two weeks since,
How've you been?
We both know the answer to a question so bleak,
I ponder the thoughts of all that was left unsaid,
In worlds of thought I sit and inhale a breath of your air,
Sometimes I wonder if we were disparate members of the
  same society,
Let's take a seat and dig up our grave for pieces of answers we
  never got.

I know you didn't mean to hurt me,
I, for one thought we were a sure thing,
How couldn't we be?
You took my hand as your fingers ran over my ring,
Roman numerals spell out 26/2/24.
But that's just between us.

We went downstairs and danced at the party,
Your hands all over me,
I felt the same butterflies taking flight in the pit of my
  stomach as your hand grazed my thigh,
I have no self-control when your body touches mine.
Take my heart for now.

Western Plains

In worlds far apart we lay,
I see stars on the Western Plains,
Breath in the cold crisp air,
"I'm sorry" he whispers between shivers under the blankets,
Swept across the grass,
"I know" I say.
"Do you hate me?" he asks
I shake my head,
It's not in me to hate him.

Sometimes the right person falls into the right place at the
    wrong time,
Because who could have guessed,
That you would change your mind.
Take another drink,
Or kiss me.
Fuck it, who cares,
If it was meant to be,
I wish it was with me.

The Stars that Night

I'll never forget us under the stars,
Where your tender fingers rubbed the scars of my marked
    heart,
I wish we could go back to the start,
And not hurt each other.

On train tracks we passed,
Hand in hand,
Heart to heart,
Just two boys walking each other home,
These feelings were never harsh.

Intrusive Thoughts

Witlessly I ponder how things would have been different,
If your mind didn't change,
And I was chosen,
Those intrusive thoughts are worse than any drug I've taken
   in my friend's bathroom,
Or in the back of any car,
Naively I let
One press on my shoulder,
One hand in mine,
One smile that lasts a second too long,
One moment in your arms,
Take me right back to where we started,
Before you broke my heart.

One Night Out West

Seeing you out in town stirs a whirlwind of anxious leaves,
They twirl in the pit of my belly,
I take another breath of nicotine and let the smoke bring me
   some peace,
The boy in The Gorillaz jumper greets me like nothing's
   changed,
Like he didn't break my heart.

His kind words and tender hands reach out to touch me,
And I should know better,
I'm far too wise from memory scars to let these words reach
   the ache in my own soul,
But I let him in, for old times' sake.

Hid hands across my shoulders on the dance floor,
His fingers deep into my shoulders and pressure brings
   pinch,
Do it again,
I know now that we're apart this doesn't mean a thing,
But I let him in, what else can he take?

A simple stumble home from the bar,
I find the same boy in my arms,
Fate always works with us this way,
I lend him my heart knowing it will break.
Shortcut across the train tracks,
We gaze over the big, big world of open night stars,
This world is much bigger than him,
Yet here I stand with the same man, hand in hand,
Walking him home.

Under a world so large I chose to be here in the moment,
Despite his love being lost something still brings me near,
He's a soul mate who met me at the wrong time or wrong
    year.
I know it's going to hurt in the morning,
But that's the price I pay to be in his orbit.

Tattooed, Denim Jacket, Silver Chain

Fingers run through the brown waves of my curly hair,
A silver chain around my neck screams "don't you dare come
  near",
Tattoo artists colour my skin in their chair,
Denim on my shoulders,
Now that I'm older
I know what bad boys *taste* like.

We lock eyes in pub light,
My heartbeat brighter than starshine,
Something about his green eyes makes me lose sight,
My cold exterior trying to keep up appearances,
But the warmth of his cool, pale skin
Sends my mind into places of sin.

I'm trying to be brave in the presence of the boy who broke
   me,
But innocence in tree leaf eyes in springtime
Makes me lose all signs of distress.
Then there we were, pressed in bedsheets,
He's safe with me,

He traces the lines of my inked skin,
My jacket on his bedroom floor,
My chain around his fingers,
And the bad boy in me loses his senses.

Just One More, Then I'm Done

Bad habits stalk me down the hallway from my bathroom,
They're the mean girls in school with nothing kind to say,
The grit in my teeth and lump in my throat,
I pace back and forth in my room,
Pretending I'm not provoked,
By temptation.
Heavenly clouds and daydream artwork fill my brain.

My fingers ache for that touch once more,
Even though I know how bad it's going to be for me,
Progress makes me near perfect,
But his scent so near yet so distant makes me feel worthless,
The fumes of his breath I inhale,
A need so bad I bite my fingernails,
Self-control was never really my thing,
So from either side of my one track mind I derail,
All for the cheap thrill,
Every detail.

Bigger Than Him

Friends gather side by side,
Sip cheap drinks and offer cheap advice,
Nobody ever knows how bad you're hurting when you're the
  one driving,
Part of me wants to cut my own fingertips just to see some-
  thing external bleed,
"Just block him, cut him out"
But it's not that easy.

One friend nods her head and watches me suffer in silence,
My empathy coupons have expired,
But she tilts slightly more and listens to the way I speak on it,
It's the safety in solace when she makes a promise,
That I'll never be alone again.

Before long, anxiety is my old friend,
In some people's company there's no need to pretend you're
  fine,
"Just take your time"

She pats my shoulder like my brother,
A comfort spot for when I'm feeling forlorn,
This life is so cruel sometimes,
How dare it show me my whole world and take it from me
the same night,
Once more she inches closer and lands her head on mine,
Suddenly the world was bigger than him,
Bigger than all the sky on a starry night.

Forgive Me but Screw Me

No one actively hates me besides me,
A pattern of ill wishes present,
I sit with myself and loathe the company of television
    reflection,
And the boy in the glass cup,
Or the face that unlocks my phone screen,
How does one continue to hurt themselves,
Despite the promise of better days?
Truth is, I'm afraid,
That the best days have come and gone away,
That I'll never feel the thrill of anyone else,
I'm terrified that this was my big chance,
For all the things love songs promised us,
And it passes me by like the highway cars and their
    headlights.

Just Friends For Now?

Perhaps I'm stupid for love,
Such a bad habit to feel so intensely,
I guess that's the lesson,
If I can't have him in pictures on our wall,
Can I have him at all?
Is 'friends' a presence I welcome, knowing we've never done
it before?
We've never not had feelings that sparked bright night stars,

Being "just friends" is *access* to me,
Without commitment or the ring,
You take the best of me,
And I give it away for free.

Something New

I love that we don't hate each other,
Things could have been so much worse,
Ugly words,
Spiked tongues,
Broken truths,
You should have shattered the rest of me,
Like the heartbroken crack I left in my mirror
But you didn't.

You showed kindness even when I didn't want it,
I could have clenched the shattered pieces until my hand
    bled,
But you took it instead,
And I told you "I could never hate you".

You've never had anything bad to say,
If we're going to end,
I want it to be this way.

To The Poet

It's me again,
Just checking in,
How have things been?
Stupid question, I know,
But I can't help but ask
How's your social mask?
Even though time has passed.

You're days older than your last blood poured sonnet,
Take a moment and think on it,
The distance between you and me isn't great,
But already you're inches closer to a far better place,

Your heart may be tender,
But time heals most,
Things will get better,
Because of this you're stronger,
And I know we're only days apart,
But I will love you much longer.

Why I Write Poetry

The ink inscribed on my brown leather-bound notepad is
   heavy;
With the baggage it carries
With good days falling so hard I crack my bones on the
   sidewalk,
Being so jealous I burn pictures of tender subjects,
And their friends,
The pages span on all things I hold close looking backwards,
It feels like the only way to push *forward*.

I sit with the pages like they're my old friend,
We check in on one another,
Make sure my heart still believes every word,
A fragment of feeling in a moment gone too soon,
It's past days we grieve,
But the futures we created too.

What Could Have Been

I stay up far too late,
In places I've never seen,
In futures I could only dream,
Tides turn on twisted winds of fate,
And the prices I'd pay to keep my fate safe.
Perhaps my imagination can run wild, to enjoy the fantasy
for a moment.
I'll drag those dreams back home to the same place you broke
them,
Then I'll blow smoke and let the nicotine make my head
float,
Next steps from here are only mapped for two days ahead,
Because all those dreams of us are buried and dead.

The Story is Me

Sometimes I wonder how I built a world around pictures of
    you,
I glance at the snow globe of the life we would live,
Wilted flowers and lines on our faces,
But every once in a while, I squeeze my hands around the
    fragile glass
Wishing it would crack,
Because the world behind glass is just a facade
I should have known we wouldn't last,
I'm mad as hell that I allowed the minimum to be my
    everything.

Every once in a while my fixated eyes catch a glimmer of
    sunshine,
The beams that glow beyond the globe,
And I look up.
Once in a while I look around,
My eyes away from the globe-sized world, I can see
This world is much bigger than him,
In my pocket, the glass ball sits,
I can't let it shatter just yet,
Because you were a journey of shaken worlds and twisted
    turns,
And you will make one hell of a story.

It's Kinda Blurry

I met a guy of the sweet kind,
And his green eyes haunt my state of mind,
And blurred eyes,
And crossed lines,
It's a friendship type,
Touch me here,
Hold my hand,
I'll tell myself it's lies,
But white lines
On bathroom tiles
And highways I got lost on
He's not mine
And its lines we crossed.

Distance

Time is a fickle friend,
It curves down the roads,
And never skips highway bends,
Tender wound healing while I'm on this journey
Has me feeling like we can't talk the same words anymore,
Better yet, we *can't* anymore,
We can't dance the same way without me craving my hands
    on your skin,
We can't talk in bed for hours and sleep the day away like in
    old times,
We can't get coffee and I can't touch your knee while you're
    driving,
That's not you and me in the way I want it to be,

But distance isn't kind to all,
Not in the same golden ticket way they all speak of,
It's not like they wrote the book on it,
They only paraphrase the parts that suit the moment I'm
    caught in,
Harsh advice for the guy whose own heart he has come to
    despise,

What a shitty habit to allow my body to tense
And my hands to clench in your presence,
Distance sends me through the forest of unknowns,
Places where strange men bargain for my time,
And other parts of me I reserved for one boy in this lifetime,

Distance makes my mind explore all those what if's,
It takes its own pictures and adds you in,
Tenderly it takes the portrait and hangs it with pride,
Nails embedded into plaster walls that will cave with ill
    wishes and goodbyes,
Its fingers bleed in the creative scene,
So let's not pretend anyone else knows where I've been.

THE MESS

I

MADE

IS

THE PRICE

I PAY

Stay or Go

How will I know that we're through if you keep coming to
    my place?
We know how this goes on the best of days,
We're veterans of this game we play,
But we play the game anyway,
I said that I'd learn to be a friend without getting hurt,
But now your unversed way of being friends makes me weak,
I go straight to my knees,
And now wounds bleed,
I can't relate to this,
I thought time with you is all I'd need.

Best Of Me

I miss the days where you'd send me video messages
    before bed,
I could see your face as you lay your head to rest,
Fuck how I wish I could put my arms around you,
Watching those green eyes grow heavy,
I would have been your person,
At least I did my best.

The Lessons I Wish Life Wouldn't Teach

From the battle scars left on my heart
I finally let go of the rope
From fear to hope
It's like I could breathe
In ways only one could dream of
His hand is warmer than typical,
His fingers linger longer than usual,
His eyes lock with mine
And I dream for more time.

What's Left of You

Some days I wish I could unrecall
How your voice echoes through my windows and walls,
But then a voice whispers to me
Softly and slowly,
"You can kiss me anywhere you like" he says,
Just like at that street party,
So much pride in who we are,
I can't deny the safety that softens even your deepest of
    blows,
Bed sheets and pillows still smell like you,
I can't sleep right anymore,
Your imprints on my heart and soul are all I have to hold.

pleAse pLease makE me a promise, Can you?

I found the love of my life,
And they say hurt heals with time and space,
But I don't want space,
I want you at my place,
I want you around and maybe then we can figure out
How to be in each other's lives
With only smoke and no flame
Perhaps we can rekindle some part of that spark
That drew us here anyway
Or just be present for each other either way.
You're my favourite person any time
Of every day.

Something New

Nobody prepares you for the pain you go through,
Sitting at the cemetery with blue and purple veins,
Half alive,
Half awake.

Your presence in the everyday feels the same,
Like you didn't walk into my life by fate,
Just for you to leave me anyway.
Maybe I'm too sentimental
Or just thrive from the rush
I feel from your touch.

We tossed and turned in bedsheets
I love that we still have closeness,
But bounties and boundaries take cash
From my pocket coin stash,
It's the debt I'll pay
For the bleeding burden of being friends

I love you just the same.

Each Day

Each day that passes is a breath of fresher air
A slightly lower pain in my mind I bear,
You're forever crossing the cracked roads in my mind
Walking me home,
Telling me we're fine
And one day I'll believe it's true
But for now,
I'm not me without you.

Sunday (once more)

The day you left,
The pillow where you laid your head,
Sent me sweet scents,
Leftover from the weekend we laid bare,
I turned over to feel what felt like you,
As if you were still there
Fuck, there isn't much I wouldn't do to keep that here,
To keep you near,
I couldn't sleep for hours,
In wake of your lingering presence
I know it doesn't make sense,
For friends to long for that kind of connection,
But I'll do my best to lay my own head to rest
Waiting for you to come back again,
Absent time flies by,
Once in every lifetime you feel the intoxication of someone
    else,
My room without you in cool, evening spells
Feels like a summer hell
But I'll behave and wait,
Until you're ready to say
Can I come over again?

If Only You Knew

Your defenceless reasons
Caution me of treason
Warned me of boys who come and go within the season,
"But he's my man, there's no one else whose time I'd rather
    spend"
And that's what cracked my mending heart,

The work I did on myself,
Like a kid learning to tie his laces so he doesn't trip and fall,
Scraped on the concrete for all the world to see,
I unlearned how to deliver those viper bites,
My fangs removed and my words empathised,
I was the right guy at the wrong time,
A man capable of giving you the good life,
Showered you in kisses and words of kindness,
I'd donate a kidney if it kept you alive.

The morning came where you broke me off,
I could have sworn the hillside cliffs looked like a bouncing
    rock,
Back to bad habits I inhale the smoke in hopes that I choke,
But the head spin comes rumbling in,
And the loss of a man who's like my twin
Becomes the only thought that I can never forget.

Sometimes I Run Scared

I drive as fast as I can,
From the hills to the coast, I ride,
My car rumbles and patters like the pang in my heart,
It pumps blood to the unwilling body
No longer capable of keeping himself here

These cherished friends gather in the living room,
Warm light doesn't usually shine bright,
But the halo glow around her soul touches me,
Warmly as winter days settle in,
I'm cold inside and out if you ask me,
But she touches me tenderly and brings me in
My friends from uni days hold me close
For a day or so I feel safe again,
Olivia holds my shoulder and presses firmly where he once
    was,
"We're gonna get through this"
And then I know it.
Thank you Jayme,
Thank you Gabbi,
Thank you Izaak.

FROM

EITHER

SIDE

OF MY

ONE TRACK MIND

I DERAIL

Sundays Die Screaming

The cool morning air awakens my senses,
I turn over to see you still sleeping soundly,
For a brief moment, there's comfort in that,
Knowing you're okay and you're safe,
Here with me you'll always be that way,
The clock strikes and it's time for you to go,
Travel safe,
And please
Let me know when you get home.

My Own Terms

I live with myself every day,
My skin moves around my flesh and bones
Don't tell me what I know,
Maybe even for a brief passing of a second just don't
Pretend to know me like a vessel of goodwill and nice ideas,
Stand by me in my pain
And bad decisions.

I don't seek life advice,
My hearts still open like a cut from his knife,
Don't tell me to abandon a man for whom I would've died
   twice,
It's not an easy road to travel on with bare feet
And a symphony of sweet hopes and dreams,
I want him with me.

Perhaps that looks different now,
Given the house he burned down
Still provides warmth and safety somehow,
Those embers only burn a little,
Even if I have to dress my own wounds
I'll take him and all my other essentials.

"I Don't Feel in Love"

He pauses in his sleep
Rolls over to check his phone screen,
Types the message that will end it all,
Presses send and that's it,
Back to sleep again.

He tells me he doesn't *feel* in love with me,
Was his head lost?
Well, what were those words on his lips that he dropped?
I could have sworn my fuckin heart stopped,
He's the one, he must be,
But he's not in love with me

While he slides into messages, I lick my wounds clean,
How can someone just move on
Just like that?
Click
The end of our cinema screen.

Radio Silence

Your satellite sends subtle signals,
Are you done with me?
Just speak your truth,
Hurt me twice,
It's better than blurred lines.

Vices

Ever taken something up to fill a void?
I could tell you all about it,
How I traded the warmth of his kiss,
For the burn of nicotine hits,

Or the thrill of those green eyes looking at mine,
Now I look down the neck of my last drink for the night,
I scratch my brain remembering his body laid on my skin,
Replaced ever so quickly with my body prepared to commit
    to any sin,
Is this how it'll always be?
Don't be ridiculous
It's how it's always been.

I'll Wait

Do you remember when I said I'd wait?
A vow I will uphold,
Words I will endlessly defend
Keep me like a friend,
But I'll keep you like a promise,
Just don't wait till my end.

I can't guarantee when that day will come,
But I can assure you I will be yours
Even when we're lost.
So go searching for thrills in dark cornered spaces,
I'll be here like I've always been,
Keeping the fire warm until you're home and you know
Where your place is

Fuck it, even on my wedding day,
Call me like it's another one of our Sundays
Just say *run away with me*
You and I both know it's a chance we can take.

It's the Small Things

I will forever mourn those sweet introductions,
Where I get to show you off to the people I know,
This is the man I *love*,
And you can shine in their good company, and they'll know
You're mine,
I'm not fine now that this isn't our reality,
What would've been
If you just loved me
If you just *chose* me
It's a promise people should keep,
Like I keep you here.

Say My Piece

I always thought it would be you,
And please believe I wanted it to be,
If there was anything more I could do
Tell me like it's a secret we'll keep.
Please please recall your fondest memories of me,
I'll walk through life under the same stars,
Knowing whether we're near or apart
You'll forever leave your mark.

How?

I struggle to reason with the idea of
Treason
How, just how could you *love* me
Then *leave* for no good reason,
But you'll keep me in your circle of friends,
For fun and games until it's my heart that's broken.
Sew your seeds,
Reap the benefits,
Bake your cake,
Then eat it.

I Miss This

In my mind I visit that hotel
Same place where you met me,
Feelings for you came on so suddenly,
You just make so much sense in the scheme of things,
How I wish you and me were meant to be,
Some wicked joke of fate
Pulls me in and makes me wait,
Losing you is losing *everything*,
Like I've lost my soulmate.

Hooked

Hook, line and sinker,
Around me you wrap your finger,
Keep your distance until alcohol tastes
Like my lips and you don't want to wait,
It's a risk I'll take to play the game,
Trip and fall for me all over again,
Just don't leave me here alone in my bed.
Remain breakable.
Who's going to stop you from pulling me back in?
When I fell, I fell so hard I felt my bones crack and my tender
    heart ached all the same,
No one grasps me firmer than you do around my arms,
I wish to remain breakable by another man's hands,
There's some power in giving myself permission to allow
    someone in,
And not let it sting,
But then you make me feel again,
Like it's always been,
Pulling me in and feeling your warmth,
I get so high that any other guy won't cut it,
I'd search streets and men's sheets,
Next fix just doesn't hit like I wish,
They're not the "you" I want to come home to,
Other guys send me signs that I'll be fine,
"Come home with me instead"
Never mind.

I TRADED THE WARMTH OF HIS KISS FOR THE *BURN* OF NICOTINE HITS

I Had to Ask

Can I please ask something?
Mainly for my own self-esteem,
Like a bloody wound I must lick clean,
Tell me, if it isn't me,
Then who could it be?
I know you say it's not what you seek,
My heart wrapped around yours
Like cling wrap suffocating me as I breathe,
Maybe I get off on the thrill of jealousy,
How you tell me you don't love romantically,
But take a kiss off a hotel host lavishly,
I ask for the sake of my own sanity,
A medicine for my own insecurity,
If you were looking for love,
Could it be found in me?

The Bad Habits Club

Welcome, welcome,
Come one or come undone,
Inside it's fun!
Chaos for the borderline problem child,
Disturbia for downtrodden and victim of lies,
Don't worry, you'll be fine,
We cry together all the damn time,

So, take another drag,
Sip from the same bottle,
Hope the comedown doesn't last,
Just don't stay still,
Anxiety shakes and chances we take,
All fuck us up in the end.

Detail

I trace the tattered lines of your worn-out jumper,
The one you got from a friend years ago,
Your bedpost sticker in the background of every photo
Haunts me as I sleep in my bed alone,
I search for meaning in every detail,
Sentimental value traded on the black market,
Like my judgement was heavy on truth scales
My heart unmatched for yours as you stumbled off our heat
  trail,
One might recall a night where your coloured shirt
  unbuttoned
Told me your love is for me and my heart nearly exploded,
Or how when you sleep your head turns back and forth,
I devoted my being to letting you sleep soundly,
Forget any wrongdoings because I want to remember you
  kindly,
Between the blood spilled on my poet pages
Are the tiny details of you no one else can tell like I do,
I'll never forget your stories shared over puffs of smoke,
To me it isn't fair,
That I'm just a lover gone rogue,
How I miss clean air.

Think of Me

Late night, and my head is spinning,
My thoughts become ocean baths filled with crashed waves
   of memories I'm missing,
I can't get out of my car without looking up at the sky
Wondering if it looks the same from your yard outside
In all those glimmers of forced smiles and happy thoughts
I think of you,
And everything I lost
Please remember there's always love here for you
Like a warm cup of tea or blanket on your shoulders
I'm never far away if you want me to be closer.

It Was Gonna be a Song

You looked at me from down the hall
Who would have known we'd get this far?
Those green eyes and
My friends ask me "who's that man" sleeping in my bed,
All of those kisses and near misses to leaving me on read,
What a charming way to end,
With good time I surmise that it's you and me forever,
Your body next to mine makes everything feel better
So what the fuck was that text you sent me telling me we're
    ending?
I'll never understand it.
If I was worth it
Your words go beyond my surface
Then couldn't we just work it out somehow?
I think versions of me knew better than to trust a traitor
But love is funny
Compromising,
Hitting me where it hurts
Wishing for sunsets with you on a beach
I'm out here stuck in the desert.

My Story My Way

Everything was left empty one Wednesday morning,
The world I built, a labour of love,
Good faith,
Kindness,
And vulnerability
Taken.

So I scratch the pages with my pen,
And recount the days leading to our end,
My duty to myself is to expel these words from my soul,
Broken and bandaged with my fist clenched waiting for your
    call,
I won't spare any detail, in fact, I'll tell it all.

Whatever Happens, Right?

Whatever happens will be what it will be,
The possibility haunts the idea of you and me,
Rekindled flames,
Playing the same game,
Ashes fall around me the same way,
I'm a mess of a man,
I'm a mess you made.

The Lowest

I don't want to be in love,
It's done nothing but hurt me,
I feel the pang in my heart
Every time he opens his dating apps,
Calls for the attention of anyone else
But me,
Self-esteem sinks like a tarnished jewel lost at sea,
Dismay for my own face bruises my mirror like broken fists,
I touch my own skin knowing it's where he's been,
I've got a lot to regret now,
I've got a lot to live without.

I'm Trying, I Swear

Cluelessly, I agree to be a friend of yours,
Unaware of the morning dew I trip and fall on,
No railings on pathways to avoid the landmines
Of blurred lines or overstepping boundaries of mine,

We talk, laugh and party,
Club bathrooms and we find dudes to help us out,
Hands go on my shoulders
I thought I'd know better now that I'm older,
But the habit of you comes like a craving
Only stronger.

Dominos

Ever planned the plot of a good story?
Ever planned its miraculous ending?
The disaster screams like movie scenes playing on the film
   reel,
All in my head,
I engineer a solution to problems I made,
Stories I only complicate,

I pace around my room
Planning my next move
All in an attempt to keep *you*.

FOR YOU

I'D WAIT

EVEN

ON MY

WEDDING

DAY

July

My birthday is soon,
All I can think of is you,
On a day to celebrate, I sit and wait,
Staring at a phone screen and hoping you'll notice me,
Please, *please* just call me.

I want to hear your voice as you think of me,
Rest my anxious thoughts and let me truly believe things will
   be okay,
Fuck how I miss those days,
We had routine, it was just
                         You and me,
Amongst the noise there was no one else I could see,
Only your smile in mismatched clothes that somehow ended
   up on the floor,
I miss the vapour smoke huffed from my bed where you'd
   stare at the ceiling then turn your head,
"Have I told you about that one time…"
And all is okay again.

Forgiveness (unsent because I got scared)

Hey there, I just wanted to stop by and have a moment of your time. I know things have been kinda hard between us. And I also know that you think about it more than you tell me in true honesty, that part is hard for me. I know you never meant to hurt me. That much is true. You never had a hateful bone in your body. Those green eyes and contagious smile wrap me in the warmest of quilts and make me feel safe from a world of hate bombs and love triangles. Your voice has a security that is worse than any other drug, I just want to feel safe and I'm taking baby steps to feel that without you.

Truth is, I don't want to do life without you.
We met for a reason, call it fate or something else completely. I don't care. It happened. You happened. That, I cannot, and *will* not ignore.

Withdrawals

I love that we still see each other,
We're gracious and kind,
The idea of giving it another shot plagues my mind,
I look for you in every crowd,
I want to be stumbling home with you after a night out.

Each time we part ways once more,
The squeeze in my chest pulls as I witness withdrawals,
Lack of serotonin in my head disturbs me from rest,
An emptiness I must live with,
Your scent and body is so close, it takes all my strength to
    resist it.

Just touch me,
Tell me we will be fine,
Give it time,
Maybe,
                          We can give it another try.

Postcard

In the mailbox you'll find memories of me,
Moments of life that felt like seconds in time,
I want to share these with you,
Reminding you of how *big* this world really is,
There is love out there,
In a world full of hard moments and broken people,
There's someone out there right now who was dying to meet you.

Poets Profits

You had it,
I want it,
We kissed on your bonnet,
Then left me on it,
So I now I write poetry sonnets
Isn't it ironic?
How you pushed me to that point,
A torture like no other,
Poetic lover boy,
My muse to use in ways I imagine,
I recall my own life,
And put it in typed lines.

Creature of Habit

I check on you routinely,
Like brushing my teeth
Or drinking green tea
I search your trail in hopes of detail,
I'd ask you myself
But it's a truth you may not tell.

I check up on you from side streets,
And the corner of your house where the pipe leaks,
I'd drive in front of your daily commute,
Just to save a park for you,

When you're cold I'm the package at your front door,
A hoodie to keep you warm,
I'll keep the light on after your night out,
Hush you to sleep when bad days scream too loudly.

Decoded

And when no one is around,
Let's just be here,
Every chance you'll find me trying anything to make you
    laugh,
Courteously taking every moment to hear another story,
I offer you my time,
Will that be enough?
Always in any way I can be there,
Love isn't always obvious in ways we show,
You can count on me though.

Laura

A journal of gratuitous moments and kind thoughts
Really do save you from the edge of time's end,
We forget what it was like to be fourteen,
School was tough but life was pleasing,
We hated Mathematics but made History look easy,

Boys from school busses used to pick on me,
An easy target to exert their own hostility,
Her smart remarks and broken parts made me feel at ease,

She took my hand through hallways,
Held my head in driveways,
Promised friendship always,
How do I thank someone who saved me?

We both know what I mean,
Not from the bullies or heartbreak,
But the ending of all endings,
Her time with me is my own kind of healing,
Reminding me that with time things are alright,
You can't replace that feeling.

Picture This

My imagined dreams come haunting me in my sleep,
The fantasy of us by the coast,
Walking beaches and sharing mornings before work,
The mundane and boring,
Dinner plans with new friends,
Weekends away with old ones.

I wished we could have fought about little things,
Like where to go for drinks
Or the best place in town to eat,
I picture you with a ring
And my kisses on your cheek,
My own fears washed away
By the evening plans we'd make
My anxiety slowly fading away
Knowing I'd be okay.

We could have had a mortgage
And bills to pay,
Doesn't it all sound wonderful?
The life we could have made.

Deeper Fears

You made promises with your fingers crossed,
Blindly I followed you until I was lost,
Now you don't sleep in my bed.
You traded me for hookups instead,
It's a memory I carry,
I know it's heavy,
I think it's scary that parts of you still have me.

I'm terrified I'll never find,
Someone new, in this world of you,
I don't want to feel, but our time was real,
So how can I put that to rest?
He's all I wanted, and he left.

What if chemicals are messed up in my brain?
I can't leave his life without pain,
I miss him in the mornings,
When I'm drinking here alone,
Maybe memories are deceiving?
I never thought you'd leave me.

YOU'LL MAKE ONE HELL OF A STORY

Things I'll Never Say Out Loud

I have secrets I keep.
I'm not proud of it but maybe somethings are better left
    unsaid,
In between pages inked for the ages I'll spill my guts,
I take solace in knowing you may never actually read this,
Maybe any kind of relationship we have rekindled can stay
    just as we know it.

I drank myself stupid each night at the thought of your
    senseless walk-out,
I searched nightclub crowds for someone to tell me they'd
    take me home,
I found all kinds of gems in bathroom stalls and in the
    morning, I hurt my jaw,
I sent you small gifts, so parts of home remind you of me,
I never let them say a bad word about you in your absence,
I defended you to anyone who would listen because I know
    your worth it,

I fucking hate the way you moved back into old habits like
    love is meaningless,
I hoped and prayed you'd call and tell me you've come to
    your senses,
I look at my phone hoping your text would put me at ease
    when I feel restless,
I have no value I didn't assign to you and now without you
    I'm worthless.

Core Memory

I'll always remember how you called me "bro",
I'll always remember how you sleep with your eyes softly
  closed,
I'll always remember the touch of your hand on the dance
  floor,
I'll always remember making bad choices in club bathrooms,
I'll always remember the scent of you left in my bed,
I'll always remember how you offered for pay for literally
  anything,
I'll always remember how once you loved me,
I'll always remember you,
As a core memory.

No Hard Feelings

This one's for you,
By a chance encounter we played with desire,
The touch of your hands set my heart on fire,
Maybe in another life
Or in this one,
We're supposed to turn another page,
Chapters, months, and relationships end,
But *please please please* know I'll still call you a friend.

My head engulfed in those unbecoming words on the page,
Breakup texts, jealousy, and loose ends,
Let me find you all over again.

So, with my fingers down my throat I purge the bitter taste,
One day I'll be fine, but today is just not that day,
At times when you feel lost, I hope you find your way,
Keep me in your thoughts, send me invites again,
See you around,
I'll love you in my own way till the end.

Wishes Do Come True

One last thing before I go,
I didn't tell you about that one time in Times Square,
But I will now.

I picked a piece of confetti and made my wish,
On New Year's Eve it would blow in the air,
"My wish is to find someone who loves me"
I wrote in black ink on the side of the city streets,
Turns out wishes can come true in moments that still dazzle
    you.

The wish simmered for a few weeks as I got back in from the
    summer,
I spent time with friends and stopped looking for my
    "someone",
We drank far too much and at times ran amuck,
Until that concert night when my wish came blowing in,
    stumbling like dumb luck.

Do you **remember** that night?
I pushed your hat back and kissed you,
The whole fucking world stopped, and I could swear my
   veins popped,
Everything made sense and everything was you,
All of a sudden,
For no good reason my wish came true.

My whole life I will walk on this planet
Knowing you're out there on it too,
Nothing will ever compare to that moment.

In dimming light,
Your lips burned bright,
In shadows, ashes and what's left of time,
I'll love you until I die.

All My Bad Habits

I'm a lover with a tattooed heart on his sleeve,
A boy who falls too hard or soon,
Cracks his bones on the sidewalk,
Damages I cannot undo,
I'm a guy of influence and predictable feelings,
I have no poker face
Or any good way of healing
I loved too hard and had my heart broken,
From the boy from out west,
Whose heart I'll always hold.
Maybe I'm a people pleaser,
Clinically insane in some ways
Forever obsessed with what if's
And if onlys.
I crave him like nicotine,
Just numb my brain while I deal with the hard days,
I cry too much,
What if people talk?
Who gives a fuck.
    I set myself up for an outcome or possibility
Only to be the man with a clenched fist
A victim of my own hostility
Survival is vital in harsh times,
Nobody warns you about your twenties.
The decade that broke me twice,

One day at a time
I will try and rebuild my life,
Some things may never be the same
But those who stay will have me
On my best and bad days.

If there's one thing left to say,
I'm the bearer of a good heart and kind things to say,
With a plethora of bad habits,
He had my heart and he stabbed it,
He didn't mean a moment of harm,
But I have him here now,
By my side,
Not all love dies,
A friend for life,
And he has me,
And that's exactly what I will always need.

So maybe,
All
    My bad
                    Habits
  are

Buried like
                  Hatchets.

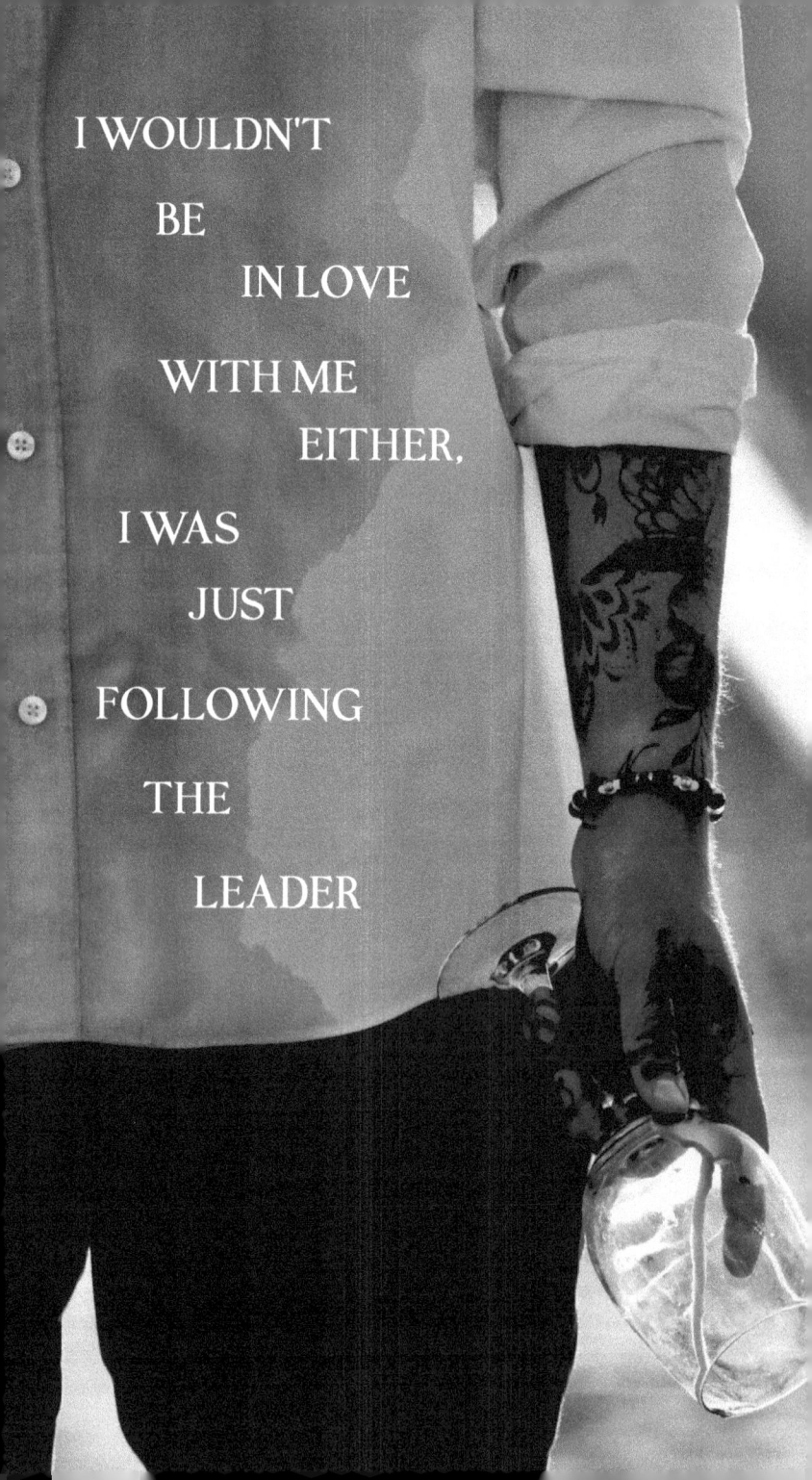

I WOULDN'T

BE

IN LOVE

WITH ME

EITHER,

I WAS

JUST

FOLLOWING

THE

LEADER

Dear reader,

Thank you for coming along the journey of *All My Bad Habits.* If there is something I want to say, it's that I hope reading brings all those ugly, complicated, and beautiful feelings to the surface so you can sit with them for a moment. Invite them in, make them coffee and go over everything. Nobody will save you from them, it's an uncomfortable dialogue we must have with ourselves to heal. Life has a funny way of working things out for us, habits and all.

All my love,
       All my bad habits

Milton Keynes UK
Ingram Content Group UK Ltd.
UKHW032005010924
447661UK00005B/293

9 781923 265424